THE REV. JIM JONES

When Jones was a boy, a neighbor recalls, "He could preach a good sermon. I remember working about two hundred feet from the Jones place. He would have about ten youngsters in there, and he would put them through their paces . . . line them up and make them march. He'd hit them with a stick and they'd scream and cry.

"I used to say, 'What's wrong with those kids, putting up with it?' But they'd come back to play with him the next day. He had some kind of magnetism.

"I told my wife, 'You know, he's either going to do a lot of good, or he's going to end up like Hitler.' "

Marshall Kilduff and Ron Javers, the two *San Francisco Chronicle* reporters who have been closest to the story, now reveal the exclusive backround of Rev. Jim Jones and his fanatical followers—his early years in a small Indiana town, the growth of his strange power over people, the often frightening daily life at his temple and the climactic, harrowing accounts of the final days inside the Guyana plantation, the jungle airstrip ambush of Rep. Leo Ryan and four other Americans, and the cult's mass suicide in a White Night of destruction.

THIS IS THE INSIDE STORY OF THE SUICIDE CULT.

THE SUICIDE CULT

THE INSIDE STORY OF THE PEOPLES TEMPLE SECT AND THE MASSACRE IN GUYANA

BY MARSHALL KILDUFF
AND RON JAVERS
STAFF CORRESPONDENTS OF
THE SAN FRANCISCO CHRONICLE

THE SUICIDE CULT
A Bantam Book / December 1978

ISBN 0-553-12920-1

Published simultaneously in the United States and Canada

Bantam Books are published by Bantam Books, Inc. Its trademark, consisting of the words "Bantam Books" and the portrayal of a bantam, is Registered in U.S. Patent and Trademark Office and in other countries. Marca Registrada. Bantam Books, Inc., 666 Fifth Avenue, New York, New York 10019.

PRINTED IN THE UNITED STATES OF AMERICA

CONTENTS

DEDICATION

This book is dedicated to orthopedic surgeon Dr. Ed Jones, Dr. Jim Perry, and all the staff and technicians at the Malcolm Grow Air Force Medical Center at Andrews Air Force Base in Maryland, and especially to my wife Eileen, who was always with me.

—Ron Javers

Our thanks must also go to those few journalists who realized early on there was something terribly wrong about the Peoples Temple. They include *New West* executive editor Rosalie Muller Wright, the magazine's staff writer Phil Tracy, and reporter Tim Reiterman of the *San Francisco Examiner*.

As journalists we owe homage to our friend and colleague Greg Robinson, killed while on the story; and to Bob Brown and Don Harris of NBC, who also lost their lives in the assault on the airstrip near Jonestown.

To be right about uncovering a situation so wrong and evil is the only comfort in this entire tale.

—Marshall Kilduff

ACKNOWLEDGMENTS

This volume is the product of a special *Chronicle* team, assigned to complete a work of journalism in book form.

In its pages you will meet the bylines of Ron Javers, who was there when it happened in Guyana and who left the jungle airstrip with a bullet in his shoulder; Marshall Kilduff, who dug deeply into the story throughout California for two years; and Herb Caen, who joins in the after-the-edition ritual of recollection and self-criticism.

Directing the *Chronicle's* special team were Managing Editor William German and City Editor David Perlman. The group also included writer-editors Michael Harris, Eric Douglas, Keith Power, Eugene Robinson, Jerry Burns, and Charles Petit, as well as Sally Kibbee, Marilyn Wheeler, Patricia Scruggs, Helen Green, and Kate Regan.

The success of their project rests largely on the daily effort of the entire *Chronicle* staff in reporting these awful events—events that had their beginning in our own American midst.

Richard T. Thieriot
Editor and Publisher

November 25, 1978

THE SUICIDE CULT

PROLOGUE

The bodies have been counted.

The final tally we are told, will be more than nine hundred at Jonestown, five more at the Port Kaituma airstrip, four in the Georgetown's Peoples Temple.

Whatever the numbers, the dead are being buried now; but many more still lie in their steel-clad caskets at an air base in Delaware. The mysteries of their dying may never be put to rest.

And the questions will haunt all America: How much can we ever really know of the Reverend Jim Jones? About the Peoples Temple? About all those suicides and killings in Guyana?

We will wonder for years about the sway Jim Jones held over his people; about his strange dominance over so many worlds around him; about the honest, thoughtful, and concerned public figures who succumbed in one way or another to his phrases, and who proclaimed that his vision of society was good.

We can only guess about the ultimate moment of Jones's power, when his followers lined up so willingly to drink from the poisoned vat that stood like some grotesque holy font in the clearing of a South American jungle.

We know now that Jones had ordered his followers again and again to practice their suicides—so all would be prepared to die whenever outsiders from the "fascist world" that Jones so feared would one day attempt to destroy their colony. But why such dreadful paranoia, shared among so many?

Some hint of an answer to that question came in a note found on Jones's body after the final day of death. Written by a follower who obviously had accepted the suicide command, the note read:

> Dad: I see no way out—I agree with your decision—I fear only that without you the world may not make it to communism—
>
> For my part—I am more than tired of this wretched, merciless planet and the hell it holds for so many masses of beautiful people—thank you for the only life I've known.

The salutation "Dad" in that note was typical of many among Jones's followers. Some called him "Dad," some "Father."

And Jones himself: What manner of man was he? What charisma did this sometimes diffident and even charming man exercise? What of his bizarre sexual life? Did his wife, Marceline, dying of poison near his own body, mean the most to him? Did his children? Did his mistress, Maria Katsaris, who died in Jones's bed of a bullet wound? What of his many other mistresses, and the men whom he loved but abused sexually? And after all the suicides, how did Jones himself die? No weapon lay near the hole in his temple—where was it, and who fired it? Larry Layton has been charged with murder. But not the murders of Jones or Maria Katsaris. The Carter brothers—Tim and Mike—and Michael Prokes, the one-time television newsman, were part of Jones's palace guard; they were all arrested by Guyana police when they emerged from the jungle, and quickly released with no charges against them. Why?

And what of the satchel Prokes and the Carters said they carried out of Jonestown with its heavy load of more than half a million dollars in currency and gold? Jones had ordered them to deliver it to the Soviet Embassy in Georgetown, they said; but they dumped it near a chicken coop in the brush. Too heavy to carry it through the swampy jungle, they explained. But whose money was it? And where is it now?

There is the mystery of Jones's curious relationship to the Guyana government. Was it only a mutual political affinity that linked them? Or was it, as Keith Power of the *Chronicle* reported after the massacre, a mutual aid pact: $2 million in cash from Jones to Guyana's ruling party in return for 27,000 acres of fertile jungle land and a pledge of no political interference with the activities of the isolated cult? And how did Jones and his most trusted lieutenants manage to run a fleet of swift boats past Guyana customs and off to Caribbean islands bearing gold and diamonds as trade goods? Why were those boats never stopped and searched? Did Jones really tell his followers, as some survivors insist, that they might one day soon emigrate en masse to the Soviet Union—to the "paradise on earth" as Jones called it?

There is, too, the curious amity of Jonestown's relations with the American embassy in Georgetown. Consular officials there made repeated plane trips to the settlement to deliver Social Security checks and other documents. Each time they notified Jones of their intentions by radio, days in advance.

Did no Jonestown resident, kept there unwillingly, ever try to contact a visiting American official to plead for release under safe conduct? Were all so brainwashed or threatened that not one could alter the State Department's view that all was serene and happy at Jonestown?

The story of death in Guyana may be over, the violence stilled but the sounds will continue to reverberate.

The end of that ghastly episode is only the signal for the start of the investigations that must try to resolve the remaining ambiguities. Even as the first funerals take place in California, FBI agents are at work. They take fingerprints. They analyze the sealed letter found on Jones's body. Congressional committees prepare hearings. State Department inquiries are under way. Even Guyana's opposition political parties pose their noisy, challenging questions crying "Shame!" and "Cover-up!".

The end of the story is indeed the beginning of another.

1

PORT KAITUMA, GUYANA, NOVEMBER 18, 1978

It happened so fast.

We were standing at the edge of the grass-covered runway of the jungle airport at Port Kaituma, waiting to board our little plane. I saw the guns. There was a shot and a bullet seared into my left shoulder. I fell.

Three men advanced on us.

I could see that Don Harris of NBC was hit. Bob Brown, the NBC cameraman, tried to stay on his feet and keep filming even as the gunmen advanced. Calmly, dispassionately, brutally, they blew the heads off their targets. Don Harris was killed. Bob Brown's brain was splattered all over his blue NBC minicam. I didn't see what happened to Congressman Leo Ryan.

I made an instant decision: I jumped up and ran as fast as I've ever run in my life across the airstrip and into the jungle. I remember thinking to zigzag so I wouldn't be an easy target in the short grass. But I also remember thinking, No, it will slow you down. Run straight. I dived into the jungle, tearing scratches into my hands and arms, knocking my glasses off my face and my camera from my neck. I was sure the men could follow me.

Panting for breath, I made my way fifty yards into the undergrowth. Then I stopped. I was in swamp up to my waist. It's time to take inventory, I told myself.

Very purposefully, I took my handkerchief out of my pocket and wadded it against my upper left shoulder where I'd been hit. My khaki-colored shirt was already drenched in blood.

Carefully, I tied my shoes, which had come loose in the thick mud. Somehow I collected my wits. Night would fall in an hour, and I would never get out if I went deeper into the swamp. I decided to travel parallel to the airport runway so that I would have some notion of where I was. I moved through the swamp until I was about three hundred yards from where we were attacked.

I worked my way into the tall grass at the edge of the runway. And carefully, ever so carefully, I peered through the grass at the plane.

Congressman Ryan was lying in the mud in front of the right wheel of the aircraft.

His face had been shot off.

Don Harris lay alongside the middle of the plane.

Bob Brown's body was at the tail.

Patricia Parks, the daughter of the woman who had defied Jones and insisted on leaving, was lying at the foot of the plane's stairs.

Greg Robinson, the brilliant young *San Fran-*

cisco Examiner photographer in our party, was at the left wheel, his body almost jackknifed.

There was no way of telling what was going on at Jonestown. Long before we arrived, we had heard stories of planned mass suicides if Jones ever came up against a problem he couldn't handle.

The stories no longer seemed so unreal . . .

—Ron Javers

2

PEOPLES TEMPLE, SAN FRANCISCO, JANUARY 1977

Up a flight of steps is a black iron grille gate. A young male guard stands inside the gate before a second door, made of wood and fitted with a lock, peephole, and burglar alarm wires.

Once inside, I receive a courteous welcome from Temple members.

We're glad you let us arrange this visit for you, they say.

The locks, the gates, the guards are all sort of an annoyance, the staff members add. You see, Jim gets these threats, you should see the letters we get from Nazis, and we've had arson fires. The stuff we do, Jim's kind of stands, bring out the dangerous people, they say.

The front hall is fitted with imitation leopard-skin sofas, smoked mirrors, potted palms, and spotless white plaster walls. Glass cases hold a jumble of political trophies—from the San Francisco County Board of Supervisors, the state legislature, the NAACP.

A quick tour sets off, and the Temple seems a bustling showplace of self-help and charity. A whirlpool and child-care area are down one hall. Off the auditorium stage is an audiovisual room where the Temple radio show is taped each week. There is a medical treatment room, a ham radio station used to reach the South American mission in a village called Jonestown, an accounting office, printshop, carpentry area, law office, and several wings in the upper floors for counseling and temporary living quarters.

Jim Jones, his wife Marceline, and their children—seven adopted, one natural—stay somewhere on the top floors of the Temple, but aides, again citing threats and arson attacks, skirt the area on the tour.

The tour leaders show off various beneficiaries of the Temple's good deeds: a teenager sleeping off a heroin overdose, an elderly woman whose illness has been cured, a man with a bad knee getting special therapy.

The tour ends in time for me to attend Sunday service. The main hall and balcony are jammed with 1500 to 2000 people for the occasion. Three-quarters of the people are elderly blacks, but the balcony is full of kids. I am given a seat in front with Jones aides sitting on either side and behind.

The show snaps open with the Soulsteppers, a half-dozen teenage dancers. "Two of them used to be in a gang in Los Angeles before they came to the Temple," one Jones follower says.

Next, a singing group. The lyrics: "People get ready/The buses are coming/Don't need no tickets/You can thank Jim Jones." The lead singer used to be a drug addict, another Temple member whispers.

Then Jones takes over. He is middle-aged, of average height, with a spare-tire tummy but a handsome, square-jawed face. As is his custom, he is wearing tinted glasses and his glossy black hair is perfectly combed.

Jones begins his sermon, a loose format of questions and answers. Aides run up and down the aisles bringing a microphone to those waiting to speak.

A man asks: "What kind of a man was Jesus?"

"He threw the money changers out of the Temple."

"What does God mean to you?"

"Concern for everyone."

Then the final question. An elderly white man asks about "the selectivity of the healing process."

"What is your particular problem, sir?" Jones inquires.

A bad back, been bothering him for years, the man says.

Jones begins to talk about psychosomatic illness, the need to believe, and then points to a woman in the front row.

"Every gland in her body was filled with cancer. The doctors gave her no hope. But look at her now." The woman, a sixtyish caucasian, stands up, lifts her arms out, and dances a short hopping jig in circles.

Several more older people raise their hands when Jones points to them. He describes their ailments and how each recovered miraculously.

Cancer, arthritis, crippling injuries from automobile accidents had all vanished, Jones says.

Finally with the audience bobbing their heads, shifting in the chairs, Jones dispatches the first woman to the back of the room where the questioner still stands.

"Give him a hug, show him that divine love," Jones shouts.

She dashes up the aisle and wraps her arms around the stranger. The two dance for a moment while the people in the crowd watch and murmur. The old man suddenly throws up his arms. "It's gone! The pain is gone! Thank you, Jim! I'm all well!"

—Marshall Kilduff

The reports you have had just read were filed less than two years apart. While there were early indications of undercurrents of madness in the Peoples Temple, last week's events proved it.

Who was this man Jones who lead his congregants to suicide? What kind of people were they to follow him? Why did Representative Ryan assume the responsibility of finding out?

3

THE BEGINNING

James Warren Jones was born forty-seven years ago on May 13, 1931. He was the only child of a poor family scraping by in the small farming hamlet of Lynn, Indiana.

Located near the Ohio border, Lynn grew up like most Indiana towns—along a railroad linking the farmlands to the industrial heart of the Midwest. The town sits at the crossroads of two major highways: Highway 36, which runs east and west, and U.S. 27, running north and south.

The Jones place was on the western edge of the town on Highway 36, just beyond the train tracks. To the east lay the center of town, a bank, a couple of stores, a corner restaurant, and the school. In all other directions stretched a flat expanse, mile after mile of corn and wheat, offering little to a moderately bright boy with few friends and lots of time on his hands.

Jim Jones's childhood was marked by loneliness. His father, James Jones, returned from World War I with a severe lung problem and could no longer work. He received a monthly disability check from the government and spent most of his time indoors. His ill health affected his relationship with his son—Jim spent most of his youth without a father.

The Ku Klux Klan, to which James Jones belonged, had a large following in town. The elder Jones, along with the fathers of many other Lynn children, met in a field east of Lynn about once a week. They wore white sheets and white hoods and preached a gospel of hatred against blacks.

One former neighbor of Jones, George Southworth, says that in the twenty years he lived in Lynn he saw only one black in town. "There was an unwritten law that blacks should not let the sun set on their heads in Lynn."

Jones's mother, Lynetta, was not from Lynn, but from a small settlement on the shore of the Wabash River in western Indiana. Much younger than her husband, she was forced by his illness to work to support her family. She had a job in a factory and also did odd jobs for people in town. Though the Jones family got along, their income was far below average.

To many of the townsfolk, Lynetta Jones seemed a little peculiar. "She dressed odd," said Doris Spencer, who knew the family and whose daughter was a classmate of Jim's. "She wasn't as friendly as the rest of us. She wore dark things even in summer. She kept to herself."

Jones claimed in his later life that his mother was an Indian—a Cherokee, he said. Though the birth records are lost, Mrs. Jones's sister-in-law, Barbara Shaffer, disputes this notion. "She wasn't any different than anyone else," Shaffer maintains. "She was dark-complected, that was all."

Because his father was essentially an invalid and his mother worked, young Jim Jones had little parental supervision. "He grew up on the streets," says Bill Morris, another classmate. But Jim was not a boy who got into trouble.

Early on, Jim showed an interest in the church, an interest that Lynn, which had six churches then, could nurture.

"We used to pretend Church, and he'd be the preacher, standing up and making sermons," recalls Vera Price, who still lives in Lynn. Jones had his pick of the local faiths. "He was allowed to go to any church and he went to all of them," a neighbor said. "You never knew when he got ready to go to Sunday school where exactly he was going."

Jones's early religious education was influenced strongly by Mrs. Orville Kennedy, who lived down the street from the Joneses. Mrs.

Kennedy took Jim under her wing, and introduced him to the Nazarene faith.

Thirty years later, Jim Jones paid a special tribute to Mrs. Kennedy by bringing three of his congregations to visit her. Twelve busloads of people, numbering six hundred people, or almost half the population of Lynn, stopped in June 1976 on the main street of the town. But as Jones got out and visited for three hours with his "second mother," as he called her, the congregation remained inside the buses.

Despite his religious inclination, Jones was also a loner. He was very changeable, always embracing a new church or going out for the cross-country team, then quickly dropping out. For a time he got involved in the Pentecostal Church run by the Holy Rollers, where the congregation spoke in tongues and whooped and hollered all night. He organized a girls' softball team, but never participated in sports himself, though his thin, strong physique would have enabled him to. As classmate Bill Morris put it: "If Jim wasn't going to be the leader, then Jim wasn't going to do it." The determination to be a leader must have been a trait Jones got from his mother. Lynetta Jones, always known for her proficient cussing, one day strolled down the main street smoking a cigarette. The townfolk were aghast—it was the first time that ever had happened in Lynn.

The young Jones also had a bit of a temper. During class, if things didn't go his way, he got angry. One teacher put it this way: "When Jim was crossed he got emphatic."

Bill Townshend, two years ahead of Jones in school, remembers, "One time Jim, who was always a kind of promoter, was going to have a carnival and give prizes for various things. Well, one of the prizes was for lifting weights. I lifted the weights like I was supposed to, but Jim said I didn't do it right. I dropped the weights real hard and we argued and fought about it until Jim's dad came up and canceled the carnival."

Young Jim could muster up his mother's knowledge of foul language. One neighbor recalls when Jim was six years old he would walk by their house shouting obscenities. "Good morning, you son of a bitch" would be Jim's greeting, at which point the older boys would chase him down the street.

But along with the foul mouth and stubborn temper, young Jones also had a bit of the philanthropist in him. One day a ragged stranger appeared in Lynn, offering his tale of woe to any who would listen.

"I don't have a friend in the world. I'm ready to give up," the stranger said as Jim happened by.

"What do you mean, mister?" the boy replied. "God's your friend and I'm your friend. And my mom will help you get a job."

"Mom" did just that. Lynetta Jones got the stranger a job in the factory where she worked.

As a student Jim Jones was only average. But the impression persists that he had above-normal intelligence. School records show his IQ was 115 to 120. "He had an amazing ability to appear to be asleep in class," one schoolmate remembers, "and then go up to the blackboard and whack off a problem in geometry like there was nothing to it." Sometimes Jones didn't just appear to sleep in class. Because of the shortage of money in his family, Jones held down a night job at Reid Memorial Hospital in Richmond, fifteen miles away. He often showed up in class straight from work wearing his hospital white duck pants.

His Latin teacher, Violet Myers, says Jim was not like the other thirty-four kids in his class. "Almost every boy had a girlfriend, but Jim was only interested in religion. He used to hold church gatherings around the high school." He took Latin because he was planning to go to college, but at that point Jones didn't know which college he wanted to go to.

During that year in high school Jim Jones began to feel Lynn was too small for his sizable aspirations. The ministry beckoned, and Jones began to espouse racial equality—a view none too popular in Lynn. Robert Shumaker, principal of the Lynn high school, described it this way: "People in Lynn resist change. They are upset if anything alters the status quo." Jones confessed to friends that he thought Lynn was "racist." He said his father was a "Ku Klux Klan type," and that he, Jim, had never seen a Negro until he was twelve. Jim thought himself a man of the people, especially the lower-class poor and the downtrodden.

As a result, Jones dropped out of the Lynn high school after his sophomore year, in 1947, and enrolled in school in Richmond, a bigger town south of Lynn, the following fall. There he grew even more religious and began talking seriously about a career as a minister. He graduated in 1949, still with average grades, and entered Indiana University in Bloomington.

Kenneth E. Lemons, Jones's roommate at Indiana University in 1949, said Jones was "maladjusted and ignored" during their time together at Indiana University. "It's a part of my life I'd rather forget," said Lemons.

Jones considered himself above everyone else, and pored over the Bible, often rambling about his religious philosophies. "I completely mistrusted the guy," Lemons added. "He was kind of an embarrassment to everyone who knew him. But his classmates didn't make fun of him, they just ignored him. We had to do that."

Little is known of Jones during this period. He kept his hopes and aspirations in the ministry to himself. But after a short time at Indiana University, he grew unhappy and dropped out to return to Lynn.

Jones found a small job as an orderly at Reid Memorial Hospital in Richmond. Within a year he met Marceline Baldwin, a graduate of the Reid Memorial Hospital School of Nursing. Before Marceline, Jones had few girlfriends. Thin and attractive, Marceline was immediately drawn by Jones's intensity and handsome look. They were married in 1949. At twenty-two, Marceline was four years older than her new husband.

Lemons, who stayed in touch with Jones even though they were no longer roommates, said Marceline was a "mother figure" to Jones. "He called her at work every day."

Up to now, Jones had steered clear of committing himself to any one church. The Methodist church had held much promise to Jones as a young man, but at the time of his marriage, Jones became disenchanted with the Methodists.

"He told me there was no love in the [Methodist] church, and said that's what made him decide to start his own church," a former ministerial colleague remembers.

Jones took Marceline to Indianapolis in 1950, and though still not an ordained minister, he became a pastor at the Sommerset Southside Church. He also took over and operated an integrated community center, and in this way Jones first united his twin ideals of religion and racial brotherhood.

But in the tough blue-collar industrial city that had been the home of the national office of the Ku Klux Klan, Jones ran into more trouble than he expected. He was frequently jeered during church services for espousing his liberal views on civil rights. Older members of the congregation objected to the outspoken newcomer —who began calling himself "biracial" because of his supposedly Cherokee mother.

His enemies struck back at him by tossing dead cats into the church or sometimes stuffing the dead animals into the church toilets.

While working at the small church, Jones lived in a fairly well-off section of Indianapolis near Butler University, where he became a part-time student taking classes in education. It was to take him nearly ten years to get his bachelor of arts degree, and almost as long until he finally was ordained in 1964 as a minister in the

Christian Church, a branch of the Disciples of Christ.

Bothered by the continuing angry reception from his Sommerset congregation, Jones quit in the early fifties to venture off again. He held services on his own in a church he rented in another Indianapolis neighborhood and gave it a new name: the Community Unity Church.

As his reputation grew, Jones was able to branch out to become an associate pastor at the nearby Laurel Street Tabernacle. But again he soon ran afoul of the conservative laity and congregation on the church board, who resisted his repeated demands to welcome blacks to the church. He quit, frustrated once more because his views were unwelcome.

By 1953 he was back on his own, working with his Community Unity Church. He tried energetically to hustle up the money and followers for his new dream: a racially integrated congregation that he could run without fear of reproach by small-minded Indiana ministers and their conservative Sunday morning followers.

For Jones, these early days of independence were embarrassing, an awkward apprenticeship. In a bow tie and bold-striped tweed jacket, he traveled door to door selling monkeys, imported from South America and Asia, for $29 each. If the woman or man of the house wasn't looking to buy the pets, well, perhaps they'd like to visit a new progressive church unlike any other, Jones said.

By 1956 he found enough new friends and money to open his church, the Peoples Temple, in a section of Indianapolis that was slowly changing from white to black. A year and untold dozens of monkeys later, Jones bought a new home for his congregation in a former synagogue at 975 North Delware Street.

His family expanded to include seven adopted children, and according to one member at the time, Jones "talked quite a few of the congregation members into adopting children too."

Jones's adopted children were black, white, and Asian, and he presented them as a strong example of his prointegration beliefs. His notions about assembling families and arranging relationships within the church circle took shape during this time.

If his base was finally established, Jones was still searching for a style, a manner that would appeal to his black followers as well as to the lower-class white families left behind in the transitional neighborhood.

He made weekend trips to watch famous preachers in action, and came away vastly impressed by Father Divine, a razzle-dazzle Philadelphia preacher who had total control over his adoring followers—many of them elderly black women.

Taking a cue from Divine, Jones announced that the Peoples Temple needed something called an interrogation committee. He made the announcement during Sunday services, at which his soft baritone voice now held forth for three or four hours.

For his followers, Jones's idea of an interrogation committee was something new, something unexpected even from Jones. But to him it was the natural result of a desire to solidify his leadership, and to surround himself with a loyal cadre of followers who could police the congregation.

The need for this form of discipline, which grew to include beatings and other violent punishment, had another explanation: the personality of Jim Jones.

When Jones was a boy, a neighbor recalls, "He could preach a good sermon. I remember working about two-hundred feet from the Jones place. He would have about ten youngsters in there, and he would put them through their paces . . . line them up and make them march. He'd hit them with a stick and they'd scream and cry.

"I used to say, 'What's wrong with those other kids, putting up with it?' But they'd come back to play with him the next day. He had some kind of magnetism.

"I told my wife, 'You know, he's either going to do a lot of good, or he's going to end up like Hitler.' "

Though Jones insisted he was only looking out for everyone's best interest, one Indianapolis member, Thomas Dickson, disagreed. The committee was "for people who spoke against Jones in the church," Dickson said. Jones had begun to change, Dickson felt, and the committee of ever-vigilant members close to Jones was a disturbing sign.

"The people would have to go before this interrogation committee and be questioned for hours and hours about why they were against him, or if there was a plot in the church against him," Dickson said.

"He always said everybody ought to love him and if they didn't, he'd get awfully violent—not physically, but verbally, sometimes cursing.

"He'd take the Bible—he called it the black book—and throw it on the floor and say, 'Too many people are looking at this instead of looking at me.'"

Disappointed in the strange turnabout in a man who had begun with simple, earnest ideas, Dickson left the church.

In 1959 Jones encountered personal tragedy when one of his adopted children was killed in a car accident with four other Temple members on the road from Cincinnati to Indianapolis. Jones later announced he didn't get into the car because of a premonition of death. He never explained why he did not use this claimed power to save his child.

Despite the odd currents noted by former admirer Dickson and Jones's expanding assertions of omniscience, Jones still remained an aggressive, courageous leader consumed by his beliefs in civil rights. Local newspaper accounts indicate that Jones and his family suffered ugly personal attacks during the first days of the civil rights era. His wife Marceline was spat upon while waiting for a bus with her adopted black son. Jones also said he received a concussion when a red-neck hit him with a milk bottle at his front door. His children, white, black, and Asian, were threatened at local playgrounds.

Jones talked of the time when he lay sick in an Indianapolis hospital and refused medical attention until a newly arrived black with serious injuries was tended to.

His plight caught the eye of local political leaders, anxious to heed the national outcry over the long ignored problem of racial bigotry. In 1960 Mayor Charles Boswell appointed Jones director of the Indianapolis Human Rights Commission and Jones gladly took the $7000-a-year job. But being in the public eye had its disadvantages for the young, controversial leader.

A local newspaper ran a disturbing account of Jones's life based on facts supplied by the minister's staff. For three solid months, segregationists tossed rocks at his home, called him on the phone, demanding, "Niggerlover, get out of town," and threw explosives into his yard.

There was also another odd-sounding ploy, the paper noted, something racist night riders had rarely done before. "Some went so far as to write antiblack letters to prominent civil rights workers, and signed Jones's name to them."

Jones spent his time, and the newspapers devoted their columns, denying and denouncing such tactics. As Jones's prominence and name spread, his congregation grew, huddling ever closer around their embattled leader.

By 1963 Jones's church was called the Peoples Temple Full Gospel Church and was a Disciples of Christ congregation. The church, which claimed to serve more than a thousand free meals a week, was in financial trouble and in danger of losing a jobs program over a $350 bill.

Money was always a mysterious commodity for Jones. Though he insisted he didn't like to take money from his congregation, he had enough to finance his travels and personal promotion. In the early stages he worked tirelessly for the church and its fund-raising activities. He inspired in those around him the same kind of self-effacing determination.

But then, suddenly, Jones told several members of his church he had experienced a "personal vision" of a coming nuclear holocaust that would poison the world. And at the same time this disturbing vision descended on Jones, the young minister picked up a copy of *Esquire* magazine. The editors had seized on the bomb shelter craze of those days to publish a half-satirical yarn about the "ten safest places to live in the event of a nuclear attack," shoring up the article with all sorts of official-sounding evidence on climate conditions, wind currents, and mountain ranges.

Two of the places were Belo Horizante, Brazil, and Ukiah, California, 116 miles north of San Francisco. Jones decided to take his family to Brazil, some said for a rest and scouting mission as much as for self-proclaimed missionary experience. In his South American travels, Jones enjoyed a brief stopover in the small, backward colony of British Guiana (now Guyana).

In 1963 the Temple and its small fleet of buses also began to travel, swinging through the lower Midwest on revival tent campaigns to win new followers and spread the word of a new skill of Jones—faith healing.

Faith healing had been the key to Father Divine's mesmerizing services in Philadelphia. A fabulous, colorful character, Divine burst onto the scene in 1932 as the founder of the worldwide Kingdom of Peace Movement. His services were rollicking, tumultuous outpourings, resplendent with red carpets and crowns for Divine, who proclaimed himself God of the Universe. All races flocked to hear the small black man preach his message of universal love and immortality. Above all, they were drawn by his miraculous cures—the raising of the dead, the healing of wounds, the curing of disease.

Jones adopted Father Divine's faith-healing style minus the rich trappings that went with it. Jones once blasted faith healers who "used the wonderful healing powers of God incorrectly."

"They [the faith healers] call for the coming of Christ and go out to meet him in a brand-new Lincoln Continental," Jones scoffed. "They build magnificent, useless edifices and squander their money."

A typical faith-healing session at Jones's temple in Indianapolis drew several hundred persons, all eager to see Jones cure heart conditions, rheumatoid arthritis, fainting spells, calcified joints, and other ailments.

The meetings were punctuated with cries of joy as Jones passed his hands over helpless individuals who, in a religious frenzy, declared themselves cured. Other followers would testify to new members how Jones had cured heart disease, removed sores, and raised forty people from the dead.

During one such service in Indianapolis, Jones called out a name and a woman stood up saying she suffered from cancer. She walked to the front, where Jones touched her, and then she went to the back of the church to a rest room, where she was told she would "pass the cancer from her bowels."

As the congregation sang, the woman returned with upstretched hands, shouting, "Praise the Lord." She was followed by one of Jones's lieutenants, who carried a white tissue paper with a dark blob—reported by Jones to be the actual cancer which had passed from the woman's body.

There were advance parties of church aides who passed out leaflets, nailed up placards, and talked up the arrival of the "Prophet of God" or "father." Among big-city folk encountering Jones for the first time, the minister modestly played down such labels, saying the words were gushed out by overheated followers.

Word traveled fast enough to tinge newspaper accounts. Reporters who had become weary of Jones's denunciations of racist enemies began to twit him as a phony-sounding faith healer, preying on gullible poor and elderly widows worried about failing health.

Jones's faith-healing activities in Indianapolis at one point triggered the interest of the state Board of Psychology Examiners. While medical and law enforcement authorities felt powerless to probe his claims, the psychology board said in 1971 that it wanted to act.

In particular, Jones's claim to cure cancer was held suspect.

A medical doctor, who attended Jones's services, told the board: "What bothers me is that people who are really sick may think they have been cured, and later be in more serious condition."

The doctor, who asked not to be identified because of a possible conflict with the American Medical Association, said that the "cancer" appeared to be just some sort of white material in a plastic bag.

When asked by the doctor if the "cancer" could be analyzed by a competent pathologist, Jones replied he had "no personal objections," but that he had to abide with the wishes of his church leaders "not to become involved in more publicity."

Jones said he was dealing with the uncertain world of "psychosomatic diseases," but his critics claimed it was simple fakery aimed at wooing the weak. Jones brushed off the official challenge: the psychology board never took any official action, never issued a critical letter, and let the matter drop.

Despite the outcry over his faith healing, Jones stayed in Indianapolis and in 1965 was ordained as a Disciples of Christ minister. His growing congregation and his growing financial success led him to try something more than just civil rights and personal religion. Jones, the poor country boy, set up two corporations.

The first was the grand-sounding Wings of Deliverance, a nonprofit enterprise whose stated purpose was "furthering the Kingdom of God and spreading the true Holy Word of God."

The second was a family corporation composed of Jones, his wife Marceline, and his mother Lynetta, called the Jim-Lu-Mar Corporation. It was not nonprofit and was intended to make money by acquiring businesses "including but not limited to the operation of nursing homes;

the purchase, sale or management of real estate; the operation of grocery stores, markets, etc."

But Jim, not known for his financial wizardry, quickly lost interest in the Wings of Deliverance and the Jim-Lu-Mar Corporation. The Indiana Secretary of State revoked the local corporate license of both entities in June 1970 for having failed to file annual reports since their founding in 1965. The Internal Revenue Service was also unhappy. Federal officials reported that Wings of Deliverance had neglected to file corporate tax returns from 1966 to 1970. The Jim-Lu-Mar Corporation filed papers for only the first year of its life, IRS officials said.

Vergil Berry, deputy commissioner of the Indiana Department of Revenue, last year told reporters the state had not prosecuted the corporations for their failures—another link in the Temple's unbroken chain of good luck in fending off official inquiries into church activities.

Jones was disheartened by his financial setbacks. Also, associates said he was upset over his lack of success in easing racial tensions. And there were the continuing attacks on his splashy-sounding claims of healing the sick. As the criticism grew, it left a bitter edge on Jones's experiences in Indianapolis, and by June 1965 he was ready to leave. He rekindled the nuclear disaster prophesy, reminding his congregation that there was still the Ukiah area where he would lead them to safety. He began to plan for the move.

But getting the members of his faithful flock to leave their jobs, families, and surroundings for the transcontinental trek was difficult. The numbers he had earlier talked of, the thousand meals a week and the "hundreds" of followers boiled down to smaller totals when it came time to leave. There are varying estimates of 100 to 165 people in the Jones party that left in small caravans to join him on the West Coast in June and July 1965.

Six months before Jones left fo Ukiah, Marvin and Jackie Swinney joined the Temple. A young white couple in their early twenties, they had returned to their Indianapolis home where Marvin took a job in an electronics firm. Once settled, they decided to attend the church which they heard "had wonderful humanitarian goals."

"When somebody's house burned down, we bundled up clothes and went over. When people needed money, we gave it to them. Jim was a wonderful person we all admired," Jackie Swinney said.

The newcomers found the church had a relaxed pace, where strict rules about biblical interpretations and Sunday school were replaced with good deeds and talk about liberal ideals—nuclear disarmament, concern for the poor, integration. The church, though its membership was more than half black, had a friendly atmosphere without self-consciousness in interracial contacts.

After being members for barely six months, Marvin and Jackie were asked by Jones to move with their in-laws to Ukiah. The Swinney family, including Marvin's brother and his family, made the drive with all their belongings in four cars.

Jones promised his small, devoted flock of followers a new refuge, not only free of the racial problems of Indianapolis, but a haven out of harm's way in the coming disaster. Who would be left after the bomb blasts killed off "all the racists" who tormented Jones? His congregation, a well-intentioned, multiracial band of pioneers guided by their strong-willed prophet of God.

4

REDWOOD VALLEY

Some 125 miles north of San Francisco lies the tiny town of Redwood Valley, a farming community dotted by weekend homes of wealthy country squires from the San Francisco Bay Area, small grape vineyards and hillside cattle spreads. The day-to-day residents of the area are simple, plain-speaking people not much different from the crusty sort Jones started out with in Lynn, Indiana.

Though lumbering has long since stripped off most of the redwoods that covered the rolling land, it is still gently beautiful countryside. Horses cluster along wood fences and wine grapes hang from rows of tended vines.

The well-traveled Indiana minister had found a place similar to the peaceful paradise he sought. Less than two months after the group's arrival, on November 26, 1965, Jones, his wife and as-and associate minister Archie Ijames signed state papers making the Peoples Temple, Disciples of Christ, a nonprofit California corporation.

But despite the exquisite surroundings, the transition period was awkward for the newly arrived pastor and his pilgrim flock from the Midwest. His followers, many of them urban blacks, made the old-time, settled, conservative Redwood Valley residents uncomfortable.

So Jones embarked on a careful and exhaustive strategy to woo his new, suspicious neighbors. He held services in garages and county fairgrounds. His people left cakes on the front porch of George Hunter, the editor of the *Ukiah Journal,* and at the home of Al Barbero a superviser from the Redwood Valley district of Mendocino County. He worked with the local community of American Indians, telling them of his own Cherokee blood.

Memories of his boyhood days among the animals on the Indiana farm led Jones to open a pet shelter. His wife, Marceline, became a state nursing home inspector, and the Temple and its members operated a forty-acre home for boys and three convalescent centers. In 1970 during the anti-Vietnam era he put up $150 to start a fund for slain policemen. "It's high time that we let people know that not everyone who is opposed to the war and for social justice hates policemen." Jones announced.

Church members, who numbered over three hundred after two years, were encouraged to take in wayward kids from the Bay Area in church-run foster homes.

In 1967 Jones had made sufficient inroads into local politics to be appointed to the county grand jury and to be chosen as its foreman. He became a director of Mendocino and Lake

Counties Legal Services Foundation, and won over the young, popular county counsel Tim O. Stoen. Jones immediately made Stoen a top adviser. Jones's followers came from a whole spectrum of local society—banks, parole officers, even the radio dispatcher for the sheriff's office.

The Mendocino County folk remember Jones as appealing but eccentric—nice, pleasant, doing good turns wherever he could, but a little strange in his ways.

An old friend from Indianapolis, the Reverend Ross Case, looked up Jones and gave him support. Case, who taught at a high school in nearby Ukiah, helped the new minister land a job as a part-time teacher. They shared a lot of their ministerial problems and renewed their old friendship.

Case found his friend had changed. "He said things like 'I'm not a Christian. I'm a universalist.'

"He [Jones] was throwing the Bible on the floor and stepping on the book during services. He was talking on and on about sex. People who wanted to quit his church were worried about getting calls pressuring them to return. We kind of fell out over all this," Case said.

Another person who remembers Jones well was Ruby Bogner, a Redwood Valley schoolteacher whose classroom was filled with Temple children, though she herself was not a Temple member.

"Jim Jones had an [adopted] black boy. He was brilliant but hyperactive. I talked to Jim Jones about his son and asked if there was any way to discipline or speak to the boy.

"Mr. Jones called me back and told me I was prejudiced," she said. But later she received a cake from Jones and a warm letter praising her for being "such a marvelous teacher," Bogner said.

The Temple kids stayed together during recess and segregated themselves after school hours. When she tried talking with her young elementary-school students, Bogner said, "they lied or were evasive about what they did at home. Then I heard there were guards around the Temple church and dogs along the fences.

"I thought all this protection was ridiculous. But if you tried to talk to the kids about it all you got was talk about what a wonderful man Jim Jones was," she said.

There was also Jones's interest in voting and elections. It was a natural extension of his proclaimed goals of social betterment, yet it was remarkable to see the direct strength that this newcomer had, presumably with no more hold than a Sunday sermon. His strength was pegged at three hundred to four hundred votes by the late sixties, and in a small by-election when the turnout was as low as twenty-five hundred, Jones commanded the largest identifiable bloc of votes.

"I could show anybody the tallies by precinct and pick out the Jones vote," said County Supervisor Barbero. "You don't see anything like that around here."

There were other aspects of the Temple that people noticed. The church constantly complained about attacks by vandals and night riders. Members said Temple enemies were flinging dead cats and dogs on the Temple front lawn or shooting out windows. Other enemies attacked the church's progressive stands and racially integrated following.

Jones's new friend George Hunter, at the local newspaper in Ukiah, was sympathetic to the liberal-minded newcomer and accommodated him with friendly news coverage. "Local Group Suffers Terror in the Night" was a headline over a typical report on the Temple.

But Sheriff Tom Jondahl said the Redwood Valley Temple "was not a major law enforcement problem. We got no more complaints from them than anyone else."

If the church had problems getting along, they were not all due to red-necks out for a Saturday night joyride. The Temple people were close-mouthed about their doings. "You'd ask them what it was all like, and they didn't want to talk," said John Mayfield, Jr., a former country supervisor. Jones himself stayed a recluse.

The local gentry worried about talk that the Temple was expanding and bringing in more people, who would probably be black and looking for scarce jobs.

Yet Jones's fortunes continued to prosper. He found enough money to build a new church with a star-shaped stained-glass window above the altar, a forty-one-foot indoor baptismal swimming pool, a new parsonage, and an asphalt parking lot large enough to line up his fleet of eleven used Greyhound buses.

He began to feel restless in his prophesized paradise. Constrained in his rural refuge, he decided to reach out. He planned a road show, taking his congregation on grueling weekend trips. The Temple would meet in the early evening at the Redwood Valley church and board the buses for San Francisco. Before the members arrived, Jones's advance men had blanketed San Francisco's Fillmore and Bayview districts with leaflets, using the same techniques they learned in their Indiana forays.

> PASTOR JIM JONES . . . Incredible! . . . Miraculous! . . . Amazing! . . . The Most Unique Prophetic Healing Service You've Ever Witnessed! Behold the Word Made Incarnate In Your Midst!
>
> God works as tumorous masses are passed in every service . . . Before your eyes, the crippled walk, the blind see!
>
> Scores are called out of the audience in each service and told the intimate (but never embarrassing) details of their lives that only God could reveal!
>
> Christ is made real through the most precise revelations and the miraculous healings in this ministry of His servant, Jim Jones!
>
> This sane spiritual healing ministry does not oppose medical science in any way. In fact, it is insisted that all regular members have yearly medical examinations and cooperate fully with their physicians.
>
> See God's Supra-Natural Works Now!

There were bands, gospel singing, dancing, and then a long, impassioned sermon by Jones, who made sunglasses and a satin-finished robe his trademark. His aides, often in red shirts and black ties, were arrayed on either side. At the height of the service Jones would perform his most convincing feat.

An elderly woman, usually black, would hobble down the aisle beseeching Jones for help. Was there nothing he could do for her, a hopeless cripple injured by a vicious white driver who had left her for dead?

Jones would be visibly bothered by this unfortunate woman trapped into her own racism by another's, and he would try to calm her. "Not all whites are like that. You shouldn't judge the others because of your own misfortune. There must be love in our lives," Jones would plead.

Then Jones or one of his aides would ask her to step forward. He would hug her gently or touch an injured leg or arm.

Instantly the woman would leap up, her limbs cured. She would toss away her crutch, dancing in a circle. Then she would run up the aisles for all the startled, first-time visitors to see.

Jones never seemed to fail—invariably the cure would be spectacular, bewildering, mystifying. Few, if any, of those who were allowed to witness these "miracles" doubted their veracity.

When the session ended, the busy Temple aides scurried around the hall, reminding newcomers when the next session would be, asking their addresses or names of friends, and collecting donations from the regular members.

More often than not Jones chose to pack up his congregation, musicians, and aides and drive on to Los Angeles for a second show in another rented hall. If it meant staying overnight, Jones bedded his followers in the homes of southern

California Temple members, with the bodies crammed so close together it was hard to see the floor.

On other occasions, Jones and his staff would invite potential converts from San Francisco and Los Angeles up to Redwood Valley, sending empty buses down to the cities and bringing back the hoped-for recruits.

One of these Redwood Valley weekends was the subject of a splashy series that ran in the *San Francisco Examiner* in September 1972. The paper's hard-charging religion writer Lester Kinsolving attacked Jones for his published claim that he returned to life "more than 40 persons . . . people stiff as a board, tongues hanging out, eyes set, skin graying and all vital signs absent."

As if such grotesque claims weren't enough, suggested Kinsolving, there was Jones himself, "a darkly handsome part Cherokee . . . clad in a white turtleneck sweater, a pulpit gown and dark glasses. He was seated on a cushion-covered stool behind the podium—which is an important necessity, given the five- and six-hour length of his services."

Kinsolving was also disturbed by another Temple habit. Aides who marched around the church parking lot had pistols and guns, or as the reporter described it, "The Prophet travels with impressively armed body guards."

Questioned about this, church attorney Eugene Chaikin said the guns were the result of the church's experience with threats and vandalism.

Jones himself said that he preferred not to

have any security guards, but that his board of directors—a personally selected group of long-time, dedicated followers—had overruled him, leaving him no choice.

The church was hurt by the tone of Kinsolving's accounts, and Jones sent down scores of followers to picket the paper for two days.

Eventually Jones sat down for a rambling, 2½-hour interview with three *Examiner* editors, acknowledging that he had performed forty-three "revivals." According to the interview published in that paper, he also talked on the special role he had assumed in balancing the life and death of his believers.

QUESTION: What is your idea of spiritual healing?

JONES: Certainly when you hear in medical science of a man telling his heart when to die, there's a whole lot going up here [indicating his head] that we can use. We're only using about 5 percent of it. And I like to think of myself as a kind of motivator. I think that'd be the fairest word for it.

Q: A director of the Temple says you've raised forty-three dead people.

JONES: I guess there has been forty-three of these revivals.

Q: Isn't this an unusual number of people to die in one church?

JONES: In view of the fact that people come to a healing ministry who are on their last legs—which I try to discourage—but in spite of it, they'll bring in people in the most horrible condition. On stretchers. Some of these have happened on stretchers. I had one eighty-four years old.

It's a horrible number, forty-three.

Q: You say you've never failed yet—that in forty-three attempted resurrections you've succeeded forty-three times. That is, no one has died . . .

JONES: Yes.

Q: In sports terminology, that's like pitching a no-hitter. The implication in this is that you can keep it up, you and your people could somehow live forever. As soon as somebody died, you'd raise him.

JONES: We can all look in the mirror, you know. We haven't evolved that far. . . . If there's some dimension the mind can conquer, I'm all for pursuing it. . . .

Q: All these resurrections happened inside the church?

JONES: Yes, inside the church. We have had a very good ratio—in the last few years we've not had a death of any who follow our beliefs.

The sensational *Examiner* series, and the open scoffing at his claims, appeared to sour Jones on the media and any public appearances that he could not control. In 1974, Steve Caravello, a reporter for the weekly *Mendocino Grapevine*, arranged an interview for a feature on local religious communities.

Jones's reaction was openly hostile. The minister was suspicious of Caravello, and accused the reporter of maligning him. When Caravello took photographs, Temple aides became furious when he refused to turn over the film.

What about all the stories of faith healing? Caravello persisted. There was even a rumor that an assailant sprang up at one service and shot Jones point-blank in the chest. There was a bloody scene while Jones was led off the podium, but he returned within five minutes, wearing an immaculate white shirt with a small bullet-sized tear, Caravello said. Did it happen that way?

Jones would only smile. "People will say anything, I guess," he said.

5

SAN FRANCISCO

By 1970 Jones was ready to move his church south to San Francisco. Redwood Valley was too small, too parochial, and too hostile to his ways. In San Francisco lay the promise of even greater successes—the city's black population would be drawn by his message, and his own political power would be enhanced. Many of his followers already lived in the Bay Area, and the move seemed a natural one.

In September 1972 Jones bought an empty auditorium at 1859 Geary Boulevard for $122,500 and began moving his headquarters. The Temple reported $165,240 in local contributions and $42,637 in "outreach"—a special category whose meaning only Jones and his inner circle of advisers knew.

Once again Jones found himself the new minister in town and he decided to make friends.

One of them was Reverend George Bedford of the Macedonia Missionary Baptist Church.

Jones learned that Bedford had run an ad in the papers suggesting black and whites worship together. Jones phoned him and brought a dozen followers to the next service.

The next Sunday Jones arrived with over a hundred people. Bedford gratefully offered to visit the Jones church in Mendocino and made the trip three times.

Bedford, one of the city's most respected black churchmen, was a little uneasy at Jones's faith healing as demonstrated at the Redwood Valley church. But Bedford found his new friend a busy, conscientious sort and Jones did have a well-integrated congregation.

"There were a few things he did, however, that I wouldn't call brotherly love," Bedford said.

It turned out that Jones was wooing some of Bedford's church members into joining the Peoples Temple. Jones was bad-mouthing the minister as well. "I decided to stay on my side of the street and let him do the same," Bedford said.

Jones launched a new policy toward the press —total flattery. In January 1973 he awarded $4400 in grants to twelve newspapers, a television station, and a newsmagazine. The state's largest papers, the *San Francisco Chronicle* and the *Los Angeles Times*, each received the largest awards of $500. The *Chronicle* donated its prize money to Sigma Delta Chi, a professional journalism society.

The church, in announcing the awards, described itself as having 7500 members. The money, the Temple said, should be used "in the defense of a free press."

In August 1973 a mysterious fire gutted the Geary Boulevard Temple in San Francisco. Church officials told fire department investigators that usually about forty students would have been asleep, but Jones had a premonition "that something like this was going to happen." So he had taken the students, along with the regular troop of followers, to Redwood Valley for Wednesday evening services. No one was killed or injured.

Jones's reputation as a prophet and provider spread before him. People could count on him, no matter what the problem.

On November 8, 1973, Christopher Lewis, who had relatives in the Temple, shot and killed Rory Hithe in an angry rivalry over Fillmore antipoverty politics. The shooting took place in full view of a room full of people. Lewis, a former heroin addict with a criminal record and a reputation as a street tough, retained well-known trial attorney James Martin MacInnis.

For a fee of over twenty thousand dollars MacInnis won an acquittal on grounds of self-defense. Lewis's wife and mother-in-law both were members of Peoples Temple, and MacInnis said the courtroom was filled with twenty to thirty members each day of the trial.

"Lewis paid me, but I understand the money came from him [Jones]," MacInnis said.

In 1974 Lewis went to work as one of Jones's bodyguards. But in 1977 Lewis was murdered.

Police called it a killing by an unknown assailant. Lewis had over $1000 in cash left in his pockets. There was no firm link between the church and Lewis's death, and there were no arrests.

Jones's future continued to expand and with it the size and wealth of his congregation. He opened another church in Los Angeles, buying an old synagogue at 1366 South Alvarado Street.

He began flying around the country with a retinue of bodyguards and aides, talking to ministers in Detroit, Houston, and St. Louis. He increased his fleet of used Greyhounds to thirteen. When Jones went on vacation, he took along several hundred followers aboard the buses to places like Mexico, Disneyland, and Washington, D.C., where they were photographed on the Capitol steps and were written up in a flattering editorial in the *Washington Post*.

Brotherhood Records was founded on July 13, 1973, as a church subsidiary that produced and sold music by the Temple's "large interracial youth choir and orchestra."

Jones began publishing a 6-to-8-page newspaper called the *Peoples Forum* with a circulation claimed to be in excess of 300,000, although the actual press run was closer to 60,000. Jones had the good sense to print the paper on printing presses owned by Dr. Carlton Goodlett, a San Francisco black publisher who had earlier won a $300 press freedom award from Jones.

The paper was a strange amalgam of political causes, church news, news from the parapsychology front, and horror pictures of German concentration camps and Ku Klux Klan rallies. There were other stories on the plight of baby seals and South American killer bees. The writing style was stilted rhetoric featuring the "starving masses" and their "unrelenting" champion, Jim Jones.

The Temple bought thirty minutes of broadcast time every Saturday from 11:00 to 11:30 a.m. on KFAX, a religious radio station. Topics that Jones batted around with his aides included South Africa, the arms race, and the causes of crime.

During this time Jones had his first involvement with Guyana since his earlier South American visit there. Operation Breadbasket was designed to help clothe and feed the poor in the former British colony. Jones embarked on a quick tour of the jungle and came back with stories of starving children and homeless families. "For two thousand dollars," he said, "you can buy a home for thirteen people. For two hundred dollars you can buy an acre of jungle land. And for twenty dollars you can buy five rakes."

Jones began sending his followers on political errands, usually the kind where bodies counted more than finesse.

One Democratic party worker found herself caught short while preparing a Rosalynn Carter appearance in September 1976. A big crowd was needed in a hurry, so the organizer put a call in to Jones.

The rally was due to start at 8:00 p.m. By 6:30 the Temple buses had dropped off 750 people at the Market Street rally site. "You should have seen it—old ladies on crutches, whole families. Then we started to notice things like the bodyguards," the organizer remembered.

"The Secret Service guys were having fits. They wanted to know who all these black guys were standing in corners with their arms crossed," she said.

Jones was given a place on the platform with a lot of big-name Democrats. During the speeches the Jones crowd was polite and mildly enthusiastic. But when Jones finished his talk, the response was deafening. "It was pretty embarrassing," the woman said.

The next day the rally's organizers received more than a hundred letters. "They were really all the same. 'Thanks for the rally, and say, that Jim Jones was so inspirational.' Look, we never get mail, so we notice even one letter, but a hundred? And they had to be mailed before the rally even started in order to arrive the next day," she said.

The Jones letter-writing blizzard was felt elsewhere. Letters arrived at the *San Francisco Chronicle* and *Examiner* whenever his name appeared in the papers. They were short, handwritten notes on inexpensive, flowery stationery, all saying the same thing: Jim Jones is doing wonderful things and thank you for mentioning it.

San Francisco talk-show host Jim Dunbar booked Jones for a show on faith healing after Dunbar received thirty to forty letters at a time mentioning the minister's powers. When the show went on the air, "Zowie, the switchboard was flooded. It was all Jones people," Dunbar said.

During the close race for mayor in December 1975, some eight hundred Peoples Temple members worked to get out the vote in precincts where winning candidate George Moscone received up to a 12 to 1 margin. "They are well dressed, polite, and they're also registered to vote," said one Moscone campaign official.

"Everybody talks about the labor unions and their power, but Jones turns out the troops," he added.

After the election Jones turned down an appointment to the Human Rights Commission, but on October 18, 1976, he was nominated to a seat on the Housing Authority commission and later confirmed. He moved up to chairman the following February 24, after Moscone cleared away opposition with calls to other commission members.

He regularly brought along a hundred followers to the Housing Authority meeting, although these sessions were usually sleepy affairs full of financial reports and bureaucratic twaddle. The Jones crowd—usually elderly black women in thick overcoats and floppy wool hats—sat quietly or dozed off. Afterward they lined up on the sidewalk outside and waited for a pair of Temple buses to take them home.

Another politician favored by Jones was Joe Freitas, newly elected district attorney of San Francisco in November 1975. At Jones's suggestion, Tim Stoen, one of Jones's brightest lieutenants and Mendocino County counsel, applied for a post as an assistant district attorney to Freitas. The new district attorney, who had made a major campaign promise of hiring minorities and women for his new team, relented in the case of Stoen, a white male, and gave him a job.

Freitas has claimed he hired Stoen only on the strength of the young attorney's strong record and admiring recommendations. "I didn't know Tim was a member of Peoples Temple until after he came to work, and anyone who says it was a political payoff is a liar," Freitas said. But for Jones the move was a further step in his expanding role in San Francisco political life, and Freitas continued to appear occasionally at Temple services.

More and more state leaders began arriving at the Temple's Sunday services. Governor Jerry Brown spoke to several thousand, and a half-dozen lesser state officials made a point of asking for a chance to speak at the Temple if their campaigns needed a lift. "In a tight race like the ones [Mayor] George [Moscone] or Freitas or [Sheriff Richard] Hongisto had, forget it without Jones," said State Assemblyman Willie Brown, whose San Francisco home base included the Temple.

Jones was never one to stick with just one cause when there were others crying out for him. He gave money to the Telegraph Hill Neighborhood Center, a senior citizen escort service in the Tenderloin district, and to a pet hospital behind in its rent. The NAACP, Angela Davis, and Dennis Banks all received donations. Jones was everywhere, doing everything.

On September 25, 1976, Jones found time to throw a testimonial party for himself, a glittering affair at the Geary Boulevard Temple, which had been rebuilt after the fire. The honored guests who were invited included Lieutenant Governor Mervyn Dymally, San Francisco brother Congressmen John and Phil Burton, prominent State Assemblyman Willie Brown, Jones's publisher Carlton Goodlett, and Mayor Moscone, liberal Democrats all.

When it came time for newly elected president Jimmy Carter's inauguration, Jones sent seven busloads of followers to Washington while he and his aides flew ahead for the special rally. Jones had been invited by a grateful Rosalynn Carter, whose staff remembered the happy photogenic crowd Jones provided several months earlier.

In the spring of 1977, Berkeley political organizer Stephanie Allan was asked her opinion of Jones. "I've never heard of people courting the left the way Jones does. Everywhere you go, you hear his name and people are asking what he is all about," she said.

"He comes into a room, gives a speech and leaves with his three hundred people," Allan said. "It's pretty strange. His followers are so single-minded."

Another political worker was grateful for a rousing reception at the Temple during the Senate campaign by liberal Tom Hayden in 1976. But he noticed signs that "Jones was no plain old populist reverend.

"We were searched with metal detectors when we went over to set up. Then I began to realize that they were there for Jones, not Tom. They had no sense of people, they don't laugh."

But few people talked out loud against Jones. He was powerful in the community and a useful asset whom nearly everyone had come to admire. What did it matter if he turned up at rallies and services with bodyguards, aides, and his lawyer? So what if the double gates to the Temple were kept locked and casual visits were discouraged? The talk about faith healing and all-day sermonizing, well, it was a midwestern tradition, wasn't it?

On the other hand, there were Jones's good deeds, unaccountably generous, freely dispensed to everyone without a thought of repayment. Perhaps there was no better definition of a Christian.

He was an untiring man who paid no mind to the enormous burdens he had chosen to shoulder. There was a wave of sympathy when it was reported he had collapsed from exhaustion after a Housing Authority meeting on March 24, 1977.

Jones's Temple member lawyer Eugene Chaikin said the minister had been up all night before the housing session in order to counsel a church member with a serious drug problem. Jones had rested for about an hour surrounded by a score of worried aides and bodyguards, but seemed chipper when he left for the meeting.

This kind of news silenced Jones's skeptics.

Some might say Jones ruled in an airless realm, a place where few but his approved followers lived. But Willie Brown, the savvy Fillmore district politician who was a loyal admirer, declared, "San Francisco should have ten more Jim Joneses."

6

INSIDE THE PEOPLES TEMPLE: EX-MEMBERS SPEAK OUT

The first signs of serious problems for the Peoples Temple in its San Francisco stronghold began to appear in early 1977.

Reporters were beginning to press for interviews with Jones, asking for more details about the man behind the dark glasses who never took a step without his entourage. "The guy looked like Haile Selassie at the United Nations," one newsman joked.

There were also stories that no one could prove about an unusual paternity suit being prepared by a married woman in the upper ranks of the church that would name Jones as the father.

There was other talk, too. The church had amassed a fortune by squeezing its poor followers into turning over huge sums—social security checks, property, even a member's power of attorney, a move that gave church leaders complete legal authority over a follower's possessions. The faith healings were not what they seemed, it was said.

The cracks in the formidable wall around the Temple did not really widen until the first group of former members stepped timidly forward. They were scared, they said, but if the matter was handled carefully and their side would be believed, they were willing to tell about Jones and his secretive church.

Nothing that outsiders suspected remotely approached the facts, they said. Jones, the good and kindly humanitarian who had won over these former members at the start, was a complete fraud, a charming manipulator, a cynical politician, and a false puritan whose public piety and private life were worlds apart.

Their picture of Temple life formed a frightening sketch of a tiny world of innocent believers spiraling downward in tightening circles. At the center of every discussion with former members is the towering figure of Jones's personality. It was he who had betrayed the former members and on whom they focused their most bitter ridicule before turning to other subjects. It all sounded so crazy that few reporters could absorb all the details and it took weeks for most of these first listeners to sort out their impressions.

The "Father"

Jones was obsessively vain. His aides dyed his hair. One of his bodyguards carried a suitcase containing a hair dryer and makeup kit. His country and western singer clothes, while hardly stylish by San Francisco standards, were new and not the secondhand discards that most church members were pressured to choose.

When the Father, as Jones came to be called, traveled with his congregation, he rode with his immediate staff in a special bus, number seven. Its air conditioner was kept in good repair, while those on the rest of the fleet were left out of order to save money. Jones had a rear compartment custom-built for himself, complete with bathroom, bed, clothes closet, refrigerator, and vault for carrying church donations. His bus quarters were bulletproofed, a security touch that members were told to keep to themselves for fear that assassins would cook up even more dangerous schemes.

The double standard enjoyed by Jones extended to ludicrous lengths. Jones made a point of always wearing the same pair of shoes. But when Mike Cartmell went to take up his new chore of shining Jones's shoes, he was surprised. "He had six pairs of shoes—six pairs of identical shoes. They were so identical I couldn't match them into six pairs," he said.

Then there was the toilet paper and shampoo crisis when the Temple ran short of such staples. "Jones got on the microphone in his room which was connected to speakers throughout the Temple and told people, 'I don't have any toilet paper or shampoo. I make do. So can you.' But in his room I saw he had a whole array of shampoo and it was the very best, most expensive kinds and he had rolls and rolls of toilet paper," he said.

Another former member, Deborah Blakey,

said Jones came up with another idea to ease the crisis. "People were assigned to go out and steal toilet paper from gas stations," she said.

Sex

Family ties within the church were always kept under Jones's direct control. He ordered marriages ended and arranged new ones. Many of his marathon six-hour sermons dwelled on sex, even directing members to swear off relations. Frequently Jones proclaimed himself the only person permitted to have sex. He often complained he was exhausted from proving his prowess among the churchwomen he claimed would not leave him alone.

Ex-members said Jones had few qualms about singling out women in the church for his pleasure. "He seemed to like tall, thin white women the best," said one former member.

Maria Katsaris, a twenty-five-year-old dark-haired beauty, and a young attractive blonde, were two of Jones's most recent favorites. His wanderings produced at least three pregnancies. Grace Stoen's six-year-old child John Victor was claimed by Jones as his own, and the strange paternity suit became the subject of an international custody fight. One woman was married off to a trusted Temple member after she became pregnant. Another unnamed woman chose to have an abortion rather than bear Jones's child.

Jones did not stop with the women in his inner circle of aides. One male ex-member recalled how at seventeen he began a relationship with Jones that continued sporadically from 1968 to 1973: "We went away [from Redwood Valley] for weekends to San Francisco. He picked me up after class on Friday when he was through with his teaching job," the ex-teacher said.

They stayed at an inexpensive hotel on the edge of the Tenderloin district. Jones, the frugal country parson, even demanded a minister's discount on the room for "Rev. Jim Jones and son" and knocked the going rate down a few bucks to twelve dollars per night. The two ate in cafeterias, went to lectures at the local socialist meeting hall, and saw an occasional movie.

The affair was carried on nearly every weekend "for months at the start." The teenager, whose parents had recently separated at Jones's suggestion, told friends that Jones was helping to console him privately at the breakup of his family. Jones told the same story to his own family.

Jones would return from his weekend jaunts in time to attend to his Temple duties on Sunday. The friendship became sporadic, however, when Jones decided to spend more time herding his followers to out-of-town rallies on Friday-through-Sunday road trips.

"I was really in awe of him. He was more than a father. I would have killed my parents for him," the former follower said.

"There were other men in the church that he had relationships with. I wasn't the only one," he added.

"Jones used to say that the only perfect heterosexual around was him. All of us had to admit that we were homosexuals," said Gerald Parks, a former member.

"Then we found out it was him. He was having sex with guys. The guys, they'd brag about it right up front," Parks said.

Jeannie Mills, Mike Cartmell, and Deborah Layton Blakey—three former Temple members—said Jones would rave for hours about his sexual adventures. Men and women would be forced to strip off their clothes at the public meetings. "Everyone had to say they were a homosexual or a lesbian," Cartmell said. "Jones realized the power of sex in destroying stable family relationships. In some cults you have communal living. In Peoples Temple, Jones, like Father Divine, made himself the only legitimate object of sexual desire."

Mills said a secretary would arrange for Jones's liaisons. "She would call up and say, 'Father hates to do this, but he has this tremendous urge and could you please . . . ?'"

Jones found sex a useful tool for controlling his Temple parishioners. Couples who thought of themselves as good Christians found, after engaging in adulterous and homosexual conduct, that they were liable to blackmail and subject to intense guilt. But to married couples Jones would often have another form of advice: abstention. Couples were forced apart and told not to engage in sexual intercourse because it was evil. Mike Cartmell believed Jones even offered underage girls to men to compromise them.

But Jeannie Mills put it most succinctly: "If you were really to be trusted, you had to be fucked by Jim."

Jones's male and female Temple harem apparently was not enough, because on December 12, 1973, Jones was arrested by Los Angeles police for allegedly making a lewd advance to an undercover officer in an adult theater.

The case was dismissed at Jones's arraignment on grounds there was insufficient evidence.

Marceline Jones was deeply upset by her husband's philandering, but the special treatment he showered on her in the form of clothes, special privileges, and lengthy coaxing mollified her, some of the ex-members said.

Jones established a marriage bureau, a kind of church spy group that regulated everything including hand holding, forced divorces, and shotgun marriages in which Jones picked a mate for a woman he had made pregnant. An offender against church rules, for instance a high-school boy seen talking to a girl who did not belong to the Temple, would be called before the church assembly. He would have to talk at length about his sex life, whether or not such talk had anything to do with the outside girl.

On at least one occasion in Redwood Valley Jones forced a middle-aged man to have oral sex with a young woman having her period.

At several San Francisco rallies, Jones would work out his feelings against homosexuality. "How many of you are punks?" Jones demanded, using a black ghetto slang term for homosexual. Many men would raise their hands though there was no reason to. If he didn't, a man might be singled out for special scrutiny by Jones. But if he did raise his hand, then Jones might call him out for special praise and heighten the member's embarrassment all the more.

The commotion over sex at church meetings achieved other ends. The example of Jones's seven adopted children did more than present the happy image of a caring minister for a father. It served by example to break down the bonds of parenthood within the Temple and made it easier for Jones to reshuffle families. Parents were encouraged to move into communal homes and leave their children grouped in other Temple facilities. Cutting personal ties enhanced the role of Jones as the only major figure in a member's life.

"Sex was one of Jim's specialties for pulling people apart and making them absolutely miserable," said Helen Swinney, a former member.

Drugs

Inside a small black briefcase that a bodyguard carried were a collection of "vitamin pills," according to aides. Ex-members said Jones constantly popped pills for every pharmaceutical reason—to wake up, to stay alert, to go to sleep, to lighten a mood, to ease a headache.

"Jim was always complaining about his health and how many illnesses he had," an ex-member said.

Jones was totally obsessed with diet, Jeannie Mills recalls. "We'd squeeze into the room and couldn't even go to the bathroom while Jones sat in an overstuffed chair, eating fruits and bits of steak because he said he had low blood sugar and had to have proteins to keep his strength.

"Jim used to say, 'How can you complain about something when I'm in such pain? Look what Father is doing for you.' "

The church had its own staff of nurses and a doctor, Larry Schacht, whom Jones had sent through medical school in Mexico. It was an easy matter for Jones to get hold of nearly any drug he wanted.

Jones added dark glasses to his attire when he began to feel the strain of building up the California church. But the dark glasses covered up his eyes, which showed the effects of his drug dependence. His moods would shift abruptly from warm embraces to fist-shaking rages, which aides also attributed to his constant use of pills and stimulants.

Guns

It was in Redwood Valley that Jones turned to showy and secret displays of weapons. His aides swaggered around the church parking lot in uniforms and talked of death threats and bombs discovered beneath the wheels of Jones's private bus.

The guns were always described—to members and outsiders alike—as a precaution reluctantly agreed to by Jones. But Jones had taken the extra step of ordering his bodyguards and inner circle to obtain concealed weapons permits. (California law requires that anyone wishing to carry or transport a weapon out of immediate view be licensed by local authorities.)

Such permits are nearly impossible to obtain in most counties. In San Francisco, for example, there are probably less than a half dozen, and they are usually issued to people such as judges or prosecuting attorneys who fear revenge from criminals.

But in Mendocino County Jones was able to line up at least a dozen permits, according to former member Wayne Pietila, who still carries an out-of-date permit issued him by the Mendocino County sheriff's department.

"When we went down to San Francisco and Los Angeles we were supposed to stand in different parts of the room, posing as bodyguards and occasionally letting our guns show," Pietila said. At various times he handled a 357 magnum revolver and a 12-gauge automatic shotgun.

"We used to practice with our weapons," Pietila said. Jones had ordered that a supply be hidden away in caves near the Redwood Valley Temple. He kept a .38 caliber handgun within reach on the podium. Visions of a nuclear holocaust faded in favor of a new imminent threat —a race war in which whites in power would turn fascist and ship off America's blacks to German-style concentration camps. The church had to be ready to fight, Jones urged his followers.

Pietila's stocky body and full face have a resemblance to Jones. On a 1974 summertime swing through Texas, Jones plunged into one of his fearful moods. He ordered Pietila to be made up in minister's robes and dark glasses and his hair dyed black—producing, in effect, a counterfeit Jones. The idea was for Pietila to enter a church hall surrounded by Jones's familiar entourage. That way, Jones said, the assassins who were waiting would fire first at Pietila. The Temple guards could then spot the gunmen and capture them.

"What if I'm shot?" the worried Pietila wanted to know. "Don't worry, I appreciate your dedication," Jones replied.

Jones also ordered uniforms for Temple members: red shirts, black ties, and slacks for the men and red shirts and long black skirts for the women. They were worn on special members-only services in San Francisco and Redwood Valley.

Most ex-members guessed that Jones had a secret stockpile of guns in the San Francisco Temple. But the clandestine arsenal was never revealed.

The Temple Hierarchy

At the top of the church empire was, of course, Jones, whose rule was unquestioned. There was no such thing as a vote of the Temple board going against him, nor could anyone expect to talk Jones out of a plan he was set on.

Surrounding him were perhaps a dozen to twenty inner circle advisers, a majority of them white women. Beneath this second level was a third, the planning commission, composed of some one hundred church principals. Within this last group was an elite circle of about a dozen "secretaries" and "counselors." Though the church was 70 to 80 percent black, probably two-thirds of the upper-echelon leaders were white.

"P.C." meetings were the heart of Temple business and strategy sessions. Jones would preside from his podium during midweek evening meetings. By the early 1970s these sessions became all-night marathons.

The subject of meetings could be almost anything. Typical topics were how to handle a troublesome press reporter; what to do about supplies for the Guyana mission; or how many people could go on next weekend's trip to Los Angeles.

Jones spent most of his time at such meetings presiding over "catharsis" sessions, long interludes when P.C. members were expected to be "on the floor." What this meant for the average planning commission member was a grueling spell of emotional dissection by other followers. Why did she wear such new clothes when there were millions of people starving? Wasn't it true that he wanted to make love to another man's wife? Admit it! How could anyone complain about working until dawn after getting off work when Father is in such pain for us all?

On several occasions, when Jones was feeling especially angry at a church follower, he would clutch his chest and scream out that he was having a heart attack. Temple nurses would help him out of the room. A few minutes later he would return to face the chastened offender.

"People believed he was having a heart attack," ex-member Mike Cartmell said. "I believed him."

It was in San Francisco that Jones let his planning commission members take part in one of his dares. He gave each of the members a glass of wine and told them to drink it all down, even though liquor was forbidden. After they had complied, Jones told them it was poison and they would all be dead in forty-five minutes. But after the time ran out, Jones told them not to worry. He was only testing their faith. "I hate that I had to do it," he told his relieved followers.

Jones frequently would doze off or munch snacks during lengthy interrogations conducted by his aides. But if another member so much as yawned or appeared distracted, it was time for fresh grilling. The pace never let up. A member never knew what to expect.

"But you always remembered to keep your eye on the others in the church," said Grace Stoen, who served as head counselor for several years—a job that, simply translated, meant top spy. "I was in charge of learning what everybody was up to."

"When your name was called, people would scream, 'Get down there,' and swear. It was hostile," said Garrett Lambrev, a former member. "Everyone related to you was required to run up and accuse you too. Defending yourself was a big crime."

The meetings eventually stretched out over the week from their original Wednesday night-only format. Jeanette Kerns-Hooman, who lived in a Temple-owned dormitory while attending Santa Rosa Community College during the early 1970s, attended church meetings Monday, Tuesday, and Thursday nights in her building. On Wednesday night she and the other college students traveled to Ukiah for a Temple gathering. They all took bus trips with the church to Los Angeles every other weekend. The schedule, coupled with her classes and a part-time job, left her about three hours per night to sleep.

"If you ever got any time off, you slept. There was hardly a night alone," Grace Stoen said.

Beatings

Planning commission meetings as well as general church sessions were the occasion for discipline that went beyond verbal chastisement. Beatings were a popular form of punishment. When a member was called up for physical discipline, Jones always presided over the session, though he rarely did the beating himself.

During the early years in Redwood Valley, the sessions had been almost a family affair. A mischievous child was spanked, a wayward member behind in his chores was chided sternly by Father. But during the early seventies the sessions took a brutal turn as Jones became more concerned with "traitors" and defectors in his midst who might be leaving.

Children were paddled with a flat board called the "board of education." Former member Mike Cartmell said one youngster screamed until he dropped unconscious.

Jones would stand to the side of the beatings conducted on stage, sometimes calling out the strokes of the paddle. At the end of the beating, the victim would hobble over to Jones and mumble, "Thank you, Father," into a microphone Jones held out.

There were also "boxing matches." An offender—either male or female—would be pitted against bigger and stronger opponents and forced to fight against the obvious uphill odds as a form of punishment. Sometimes the luckless offender would have to fight three or four opponents at the same time. At other times it was a series of bigger, stronger foes thrown against a single person, who usually collapsed in bloody exhaustion from the ordeal. Temple nurses were on hand to tidy up. If the punished was under eighteen years of age, the parents were required to sign release forms before the beating.

There was also talk of the "blue-eyed demon," a device which no one was allowed to see. It was used mainly on younger children in the church who had misbehaved. Jones would stop P.C. meetings to call out the names of children scheduled for punishment and lead them off stage at the San Francisco Temple while everyone at the full meeting waited. Jones took the kids to the church infirmary where he ordered Temple nurses to use either an electric cattle prod or heart defibrillator to send an electric shock through the child's body.

There was never any sound but the screams of the children, one woman remembered. When the sobbing, sniffling youngsters returned, they were usually repeating over and over, "Thank you, Father. Thank you, Father," this woman member recalled.

Adults who avoided the beatings faced other tests. Sheets of paper stating that the undersigned Peoples Temple member had conspired against the U.S. government, taken part in a railroad yard bombing, or molested his or her children were circulated. Members were asked to sign these far-fetched statements about themselves. It was a test of their love for Jones, an exercise to test their loyalty. After signing the one-page forms, members were warned not to leave the church. If they did, Jones would release the statements to family members or legal authorities.

Faith Healing

It was Marceline Jones's job to prepare the chicken parts each week. She had to leave them out to rot so there was no mistaking their odor. Then she would pack them away in cellophane and hide them in her purse in napkins.

Her husband's job was to wait until the right moment during a daylong service. His aides had already told him which elderly woman in the crowd was troubled by a stomach or throat ailment. When the music and singing and sermonizing had stirred the crowd to the boiling point, one of his aides might ask a question or two about the chances of healing sickness if a sick person believed deeply enough.

The preaching and praying and questioning

might continue for several minutes until the woman targeted by the aides was squirming with worry. Would Jones help her?

Finally Jones would call for a volunteer. The woman squirming in her seat, would shoot up her hand and call out to "Father."

Then while the music surged through the hall, Jones would direct his wife to take her aside into a women's toilet.

Marceline would dip into her purse and pull out a napkin concealing the three-day-old chicken liver. She then ordered the trembling old woman to sit down and closed the stall door, leaving the two alone. Then Marceline would reach beneath the ailing woman with the napkin and pull back her hand with the glistening, foul "cancer." Then the two women, with Marceline holding aloft the rotting meat, would return to the hall. The trembling old woman, her ears ringing with applause, was the center of everyone's attention. Jones had saved her. There was no mistaking the look and scent of that evil "tumorous mass" that Jones was now holding aloft. The woman could consider herself a member now. She owed her life to Jones, a life some doctor in Oakland or Compton had never been able to help as much.

There were other tricks to faith healing, former members relate. Young women aides dressed in gray wigs, dark glasses to hide blue eyes, and skin dye faked crippling diseases. Jones then hugged them or touched their gnarled legs and limbs, setting them free before the audience. The woman—magically returned to full health by Jones—then raced for the rear door before any of the curious newcomers could get a good look.

Jones had a special set of trusted aides for such chores, former members said. "Once I got to go on stage in Seattle and tell all about how Jim had saved me from heroin," said Jim Cobb. "I wasn't too bad considering I only had about five minutes' notice," he remembered.

The collections after a faith-healing session were usually the highest of the week. "Jim always promised that no one would ever die if they joined," said one ex-member. "So many nice old people believed that," he said.

Motivations for Joining

Every ex-member can remember the day he or she fled the church. Grace Stoen recalled running away, lying on a beach at Lake Tahoe and turning her toes in the sand. The weather, the car taken, the friends in the front seat, and where the first night was spent are all easy memories.

Likewise, the reasons that drove each to flee are still vivid. The Mills couple remember how their sixteen-year-old daughter was beaten until "her butt looked like hamburger." Laura Cornelious recalled how Jones tormented an elderly friend of hers who was frightened of snakes. "Viola . . . she was up in age, in her eighties, and she was so afraid of snakes and he held the snake close to her [chest] and she just sat there and screamed. And he still held it there."

But the memories of the time when they first joined become vague. It is embarrassing to recall why and how one has been taken in.

When ex-members talk about it finally, the reasons sound pure and simple enough. Jones was a kindly preacher, a warm soul with a soft baritone who called the old ladies "dear" and nodded his head while he listened.

Beyond his country parson manners, there was his promise of a new world to work toward. "He was so involved with humanitarian things. He really cared about people and would do anything to help," said Jackie Swinney.

This all-embracing philosophy of plenty was particularly enticing to the poor and the lower middle class. A promised land where the Temple provided all made them forget about paying the rest and rising food costs. It was a dream that attracted those who wanted to forget the realities, to leave their tedious jobs and work for the church.

For others it was relief from desperate problems of poor health. An older woman or man who could barely understand the medical rigmarole that a busy doctor dispensed was comforted by the patient, solicitous Jones. The Sunday morning excitement of a Peoples Temple service was much like the conservative gospel-singing churches in the South and Midwest, where many of the older members grew up.

Another reason may lie in the simplicity of day-to-day Temple life, not its ideals or faith-healing powers. Church members, stripped of their money, private life, and outside friends, had only to follow Jones's commands. Families who had traveled from Indiana with the church drew closer to Jones as time went by and their contact with the surrounding world faded farther away.

Finally there was Jones's personality. "He was a master manipulator," understates ex-member Walt Jones. Jim Jones's changeable nature, at one moment full of promise, in the next depraved and self-pitying, was simply overpowering.

Politics

Jones found the political limelight irresistible. He had been appointed to prominent civic posts in Indianapolis (the Human Rights Commission), Redwood Valley (foreman of the Mendocino County grand jury), and San Francisco (chairman of the commission of the Housing Authority). His talk of humanitarian goals and the energy of many of his young followers pulled the church toward such activities.

Though drawn to politics, Jones also wanted politicians to be drawn to him. He found himself caught in a risky gamble of trying to woo the influential without exciting unfavorable attention. The attraction was clear, however: politics provided a righteous-sounding pulpit and made for another all-consuming task that Temple members could perform.

There were always letters to write. All it took were the hands to write them. There was a permanent squad of ten to twenty young people, headed by Richard Tropp, a former professor at Santa Rosa Junior College near Ukiah. The crew worked out of a special "writing house" where there were stacks of letter paper envelopes, pens, and stamps.

"We'd have letter writing every Wednesday night," said Ruth Kerns, a member for four years. "If it was an important issue, we'd have another special letter-writing night, too. We'd spend about six hours. We'd each write hundreds of letters on one issue."

Former member Jim Cobb recalled one special campaign that caught Jones's fancy. "When Nixon was going to name [G. Harrold] Carswell to the U.S. Supreme Court, I wrote a bunch of letters [opposing Carswell] and so did the rest of our dorm.

"They told us to use different pens, types of paper, different envelopes, to write small here, and large there. We would look at telephone books and get a first name here and a last name there, to make up the false names."

Letter writers were told the Temple line in advance and given a list of sample comments to paraphrase. After each note was written, Tropp or an aide would screen it. If it was inadequate, the author would make a revised copy. The finished letters were taken by members to different cities, sometimes out of state, and mailed gradually. This spread the effect over a period of days to disguise the central source.

One typical campaign was the fight against Senate Bill 1, a revision of the U.S. criminal code backed by the Nixon administration but opposed by civil liberties organizations and other liberal interests.

Tropp called together his writers and handed

out a sheet of twelve sample letters against Senate Bill 1.

One sample comment began, "Please stop this insidious threat to our nation." Another said in part: "If Senate Bill 1 was in effect three years ago, we'd still have the quasi-police state under Nixon. Are you really considering passing a bill that would be a perfect policy instrument for a demagogue or a dictator?"

The instructions to the Temple squad were to write to members of the Senate Judiciary Committee. "You write your letter, have it cleared, and then write one to each of the fifteen senators above . . ." the instructions read.

During major campaigns in which Jones took a personal interest, such as stopping a press investigation or the Carswell nomination, nearly all church members would join the special writing team.

The weekly assignments also involved bread-and-butter letters to politicians, public officials, widows of slain law enforcement officers, and new parents telling of the Temple's good works and its humanitarian pastor.

"Everybody was involved, even those who were barely literate," said Garrett Lambrev, a former member. "If there was any opposition, such as an unfavorable article, everybody would be mobilized. In general, though, we were writing to anybody who might be of help in the future, for a character witness—from a judge in Missoula, Montana, to an ecologist."

"The goal was to get a congratulatory letter or telegram and to file it for future use," Lambrev added.

The return letters from flattered outsiders were kept in a binder file and used to impress visiting politicians and others who were unacquainted with the Temple, its programs, and Jim Jones.

But as hard as Jones worked to woo political leaders, he never really trusted any of them. He and his aides wrote them warm letters, phoned to congratulate them for the smallest accomplishment, and conducted endless tours of the San Francisco Temple with its beehive of do-gooder activities. But Jones also staged little tricks he thought would compromise his political acquaintances.

Al Mills, formerly the official church photographer, said Jones would try to set a trap for obliging politicos when it came time for the perfunctory handshake snapshot. "If it was someone Jones wanted to compromise, he would have a group of members standing behind the podium and on cue they would raise clenched fists and I would take a picture," Mills said. "They would look like revolutionaries. He just wanted these pictures on file if some politician ever turned against him." There was no evidence that Jones ever followed through on such plans, Mills said.

The tours were entirely staged by church members rehearsed in their roles, outfitted in borrowed clothes to look the part, and coached ahead of time on what to say. Then the visiting big shots were introduced to supposedly recovered heroin addicts, recovered cripples, and tough street kids happy to be fed a decent meal at Jones's bountiful table.

If a visit went off successfully and the outsider

went away impressed, Jones would switch to a new role. Jones would stand before the congregation and mock the visitor, imitating his or her voice, repeating questions asked and laughing at how the women visitors had brushed against him suggestively.

During campaigns Jones was usually careful to limit the number of Temple members who participated in phone banks or rallies. Only rarely did he allow a direct contribution to a candidate, mindful of the problem such a gift might pose with tax officials. Political involvement by a nonprofit organization such as a church could trigger a loss of tax exemption. If that happened, then the church would have to list its finances—a move with unpredictable repercussions.

Thus the contributions were small. Richard Tropp, the head of the letter-writing squad, sent a $500 check to a committee fighting a ballot proposition that would have required Mayor George Moscone, a Jones favorite, to run again at a special midterm election. The church gave $250 to the Moscone Dinner Committee, a special fund set up to pay for inaugural and office expenses.

But if big money was out of the question, the politicians were always grateful for the troops that Jones could supply. There were plenty of rallies such as the one organized for Rosalynn Carter where the Jones followers made an enormous difference. In addition they could walk precincts, patiently knocking on doors and hanging vote cards on mailboxes. The younger ones were in demand to work phone banks at election headquarters. During a state senate primary, Linda Mertle remembered she was instructed to report to candidate Fred Furth's campaign storefront.

"They told us before we went to school that we'd have to go to headquarters after school to make phone calls. We usually went twelve at a time and went maybe six or seven times."

Another Furth worker said the Temple provided about a hundred workers for get-out-the-vote efforts and between two hundred and three hundred people for benefits and other events.

The Press

When out of earshot of reporters, Jim Jones was far from being a high-minded defender of First Amendment rights. The press, he told his aides, was one of his worst enemies. He would spend hours plotting ways to avoid troublesome reporters or flatter potential friends.

After his experience with the skeptical Kinsolving story in the *San Francisco Examiner* in 1972, Jones was determined never again to let reporters have free rein within his Temple. From now on, Jones vowed, he would court the media and head off potential trouble before it started.

His first move was a well-publicized donation from the Temple's ample funds. Along with his direct grants to newspapers and newsmagazines in 1973, there were other headline-grabbing gestures such as donating $2000 to the Patricia Hearst ransom fund, $500 to the family of a slain highway patrolman, and $20,000 in bail money for the wife of American Indian Movement leader Dennis Banks.

But the most notable gesture in Jones's carefully laid plans was the decision in September 1976 to bus a thousand members to Fresno, where they demonstrated against the jailing of four *Fresno Bee* newsmen who refused to reveal their news sources.

An Associated Press reporter remembers being dispatched to the Temple after the Fresno rally to prepare a story about "this incredible bunch of people who would go all the way to Fresno to picket."

Jones begged off talking about the church and its workings, preferring only to talk about his respect for the press. "The story was pretty flattering, I guess, but the fact he had about ten people in the room with him during the interview bothered me. He seemed very protected," the reporter said. The story ran as an innocuous laundry list of the Temple's good deeds along with some inspiring remarks from Jones.

Jones not only flattered the media with prizes and picket-line bodies, but he also carefully rehearsed his appearances before reporters.

When *Chronicle* reporter Julie Smith was due to visit the temple to interview Jones for a 1976 story, Jones ordered houseplants brought in, knowing the reporter was a plant fancier. He and his aides had instructed a small coterie of members to compliment Smith on her earlier stories and to stay close to her at all times.

After the interview Jones took to calling Smith at home late at night for long, wandering discussions. He would let suggestions drop about how she could give him better and fairer coverage. Jones's staff sent Smith thirty letters asking for fair treatment. When the final story ran, another innocuous and complimentary account, the reporter was showered with three hundred letters that filled boxes on her *Chronicle* desk.

Between 1972 and 1977 the only stories that appeared in the press about Peoples Temple were reports on the generosity of the church and Jim Jones. Journalists who were admitted to the Geary Boulevard headquarters were shown only what the church wanted them to see, nothing more.

Like many of the liberal Democratic politicians to whom Jones catered, reporters and editors were given special attention.

One woman journalist who declined to be named explained how it felt to go to the Temple on assignment and leave as a strong supporter of Jones and his activities.

"He invited me into his office after the service and we talked until 3:00 a.m. about a number of social problems and broad spiritual topics," the reporter said. "I was very excited by what they were doing at Peoples Temple. It was radical Christianity."

Like several other journalists, the reporter was captivated by the Temple's efforts to fight poverty, drug abuse, alcoholism, and racism. After the first visit, there were more visits and phone calls—many, many phone calls.

"Jim would call late at night and want to talk. He didn't sleep much and we'd talk for hours and hours. It was very energizing for me," she said.

Eventually, Jones would turn the conversation in a different direction. He wanted to know what this reporter thought of another colleague who had come to the Temple asking for an interview. In this case, Jones wanted to know about Marshall Kilduff of the *San Francisco Chronicle,* who was looking into the church's activities.

"Jim asked me what kind of article Marshall was going to write," said the woman reporter. "I told him to relax and just tell the truth, but I felt very compromised and very upset about being asked questions about a fellow reporter."

But when Jones felt flattery and friendship were not enough, his tactics toughened. When many of the ex-members were revealing their stories in the summer of 1977 to *New West* magazine, Jones mounted a furious campaign to halt the disclosures. He called in nearly every friend on his long list and asked them to phone, wire, or write on his behalf to stop a "hatchet job" Jones said was in the works.

At the height of the Jones-directed campaign, the magazine's Los Angeles and San Francisco offices—cities where Jones had a handy supply of troops—were receiving fifty phone calls and seventy letters a day. Advertisers were also contacted and told to pull their ads. The list of those protesting on behalf of Jones included faithful political friends like Lieutenant Governor Mervyn Dymally and prominent San Francisco business, labor, and social leaders.

For once the campaign failed to pay off. The story appeared and Jones left California for Guyana a few days before the disclosures appeared in public. Even then Jones thought to organize a last-ditch strategy: he sent his aides out to buy out whole stacks of the magazine from neighborhood newsstands in Oakland, San Francisco, and Los Angeles, where a copy might fall into the hands of a Temple member or family relative. He instructed his aides who stayed behind to forbid followers to read newspapers or watch television.

Altogether, losing his battle with the press must have been a bitter blow to Jones. He went to Guyana hoping to leave that one very influential enemy behind.

Money

For an Indiana pastor once reduced to peddling monkeys door to door in a slum, the riches that poured in during Jim Jones's stay in California were staggering. As the church reached its zenith in the early 1970s in San Francisco, it became a problem merely to dispose of the wealth that piled up.

Former members who worked in the church's financial department chatted about six-figure sums and buckets full of coins and greenbacks collected at services. Keeping track of the church's various bank accounts became an office manager's nightmare.

Micki Touchette, one of the money managers during the early seventies, described how weekend bus trips from Redwood Valley sometimes netted $25,000 at a branch Temple in Los Angeles and up to $12,000 in San Francisco.

"Within an hour and a half, we'd get a few

thousand dollars," she related. "We'd be counting as fast as we could. Jones would demand a total before we finished, so [a high-ranking member] would write the total as of that moment, maybe $1200. Jones would then say we'd only collected $400 to $500 from that group and that was not enough. They passed the bucket two or three times."

She and another ex-member, Jackie Swinney, recalled taking the chrome buckets of change and bills into a sorting room guarded by Jones bodyguards during services.

"Sometimes, during the really good meetings, we had a half-dozen people who did nothing but sort money all day while the services were going on," Touchette said.

In the pails would be rings and jewelry too. Jones often urged his followers to donate their furniture, silver, furs, and other valuable possessions such as television sets or kitchen appliances. In San Francisco, the church ran a small secondhand shop on Divisadero Street downstairs from a Temple commune. There was a similar store in Los Angeles. Prices at the shops, ex-members remembered, were a joke.

"They were so low. Jim was giving the stuff away just to get rid of it," Grace Stoen said. Her husband Tim was Jones's top legal adviser at the time. "If Jones really wanted to make money he could have done a lot more. Tim used to remind him all the time to get rid of the money, and told him where to put it so it wouldn't get the church in trouble."

From $10 million to $15 million may have poured into church coffers by mid-1977, according to Tim Stoen, the former top attorney who left the Temple in 1977. About $5 million was deposited in banks in Panama, Stoen said. "There was $1 million that I had in my name at one time in an account of the Bank of Nova Scotia in San Francisco." Jones and his advisers, it seemed, had designed nearly every church activity from bake sales to bus rides to return a maximum profit to the Temple.

The pattern through all the church's financial dealings with its members became fairly clear. Jones deprived members of personal possessions that might tempt weak believers to leave. A follower had nothing to do except to stand ready, a loyal soldier in Jones army.

Members who lived in church communes cashed their paychecks, turned the money over to the church and received a two-dollar weekly allowance. Neva Sly, a church member for nine years, said she gave the church her $1000-a-month salary from a local radio station and in exchange received an allowance, meals, a room, and a Muni fast pass, a discount bus ticket. "If I had to take someone to lunch, I would have to requisition it a week before. If I needed clothing I had to provide an itemized statement of exactly what I needed and how much it cost."

Even the very poor were told to give contributions. A fifty-two-year-old woman on welfare, Laura Cornelious, gave her $200 family watch and some clothing and made quilts and bedspreads that the church sold.

Sandy Rozynko, eighteen, described another way that Jones swelled the church's coffers.

"They'd take a busload of kids every weekend into San Francisco and leave them on various street corners with donation cans. It was very humiliating. I felt like a beggar. I made at least thirty dollars in four hours. They made us go. If we said no, we'd have to answer to Jim and the council."

The buses themselves were money-makers for the church. They were serviced and driven by members. On summer trips a member paid for the privilege of taking his or her vacation with the church. Since the church eventually outgrew its fleet, there were crowding problems. But Jones approved one solution: crowd them in, no matter how long the trip. Three youngsters sat where two adults normally would and some even were made to lie down in the luggage racks above the seats. A favorite spot turned out to be the baggage compartments beneath the bus. "You could at least stretch out and sleep there," one ex-member said.

The sardine-can approach led to some problems. Once a bus had a flat tire on a trip back from Los Angeles. The Temple leader in charge was so worried that the highway patrol might stop and discover the overloaded bus that he ordered half the people to walk ahead to the next overpass and lean over the rail watching the repairs as if they were just rubberneckers.

Only secondarily, however, was the church concerned with acquiring wealth. Jones chose to hoard the money rather than spend or invest it. The church's good-deed donations were skimpy compared to the sums at Jones's fingertips. Nor did he live on the scale of religious pharaohs such as the Reverend Ike or Daddy Grace.

"The Temple ended up with everything I had," said Jeannie Mills. "That's what made it so hard for us to leave. We had nowhere to go and nothing to fall back on."

"It [the money] became almost a joke with Jim," Grace Stoen said. In addition to her duties as head counselor, she was one of the church's notaries and witnessed scores of legal documents.

"We used to wonder what to do with it all. But we never spent it on much," she said.

The money piled up through a bewildering series of methods. An average member—usually a lower-income black—would be approached within a month of joining and asked to contribute a quarter of his income. This slice was raised to a third and then up to 40 percent for some, former members said.

An invited guest or a prospective member would never see a donation bucket or return-addressed contribution envelope. Such an approach came later when the member's trust in Jones was strong enough to make money seem a minor matter.

"When we first joined it was all so wonderful," said ex-member Jackie Swinney. "There was nothing but kind words, lots of attention, and Jim the humanitarian," she said.

"Then it went from five to ten to twenty-five percent of my husband's salary," she said.

Swinney herself was promoted within the church to the job of handling finances for the church's "communes," a counterculture word

Jones favored to disguise the fact that the facilities were really just cheap rooming houses for members.

The communes in the Redwood Valley and San Francisco areas brought the church a lot of money. By asking a member to buddy up with a half dozen others and then charging rent for this arrangement, "We were clearing $8000 to $10,000 per month when we were just in Redwood Valley," Swinney said.

There were other ways to cut corners and shave costs, and with a little luck, escape getting caught if the Temple crossed into questionable areas.

On March 5, 1971, two social workers driving along a road near Redwood Valley spotted two pickup trucks loaded with fifty to eighty cases of government surplus dry milk.

One of the trucks was owned by the Temple, and officials found that the milk was supposed to be in a San Francisco warehouse, not on a back country road a hundred miles away.

The driver of the Temple truck, James E. Bogue, said there was nothing wrong, when investigators called. The goods were "intended for poor people," Bogue said. Jones said he had nothing to do with any impropriety and told officials he was "incensed with the idea that the church was involved." But he agreed to return the milk if it would calm everyone down.

Investigators from the Department of Agriculture and the Mendocino County welfare department recalled a few other oddities about the episode. While they were talking with Jones, county counsel Tim Stoen drove up and demanded to know why the minister was being grilled.

The surprised officials reminded Stoen that he worked for the county in this matter and should step aside and let them do their work. "I work for Jim Jones first of all," they remembered Stoen saying.

It turned out the milk came from the Community Health Alliance warehouse at 2027 Sutter Street in San Francisco. The warehouse was run by Peter M. Holmes, a Peoples Temple member with a lengthy arrest record dating back thirteen years that included unemployment fraud and assault to commit murder.

Holmes denied he had illegally given away the dry milk. Holmes said he "heard of Reverend Jones; however, he was not personally acquainted with him," according to a Department of Agriculture report on the affair. On March 12, a week after the milk cases were first spotted, Holmes resigned his job. The departure of Holmes and the return of the dry milk apparently were enough to satisfy government investigators. No charges were brought. The incident and the name of Jim Jones never reached the local newspaper.

By the mid-1970s, the church had at least twelve communes, many with over a dozen people, scattered through the Fillmore district in San Francisco.

In Indianapolis, Temple money had been small, like Jones's following. His two corporations floundered because he could not be bothered to follow the simplest requirements. But in San Francisco as his congregation grew and the money came in, it became necessary to do something about the glut.

Tim Stoen remembered coaching Jones on farming out his wealth: "I told him to move the money around. It was stacking up and was going to cause big trouble," he said.

Sandy Parks, a former member who worked in the church's legal and financial office, said Jones began to be more careful—spreading the money among some fifteen bank accounts so as to avoid a huge sum that bank or government officials would judge suspicious. The worry over government inquiry into his tax affairs became a central problem for Jones, members said. This was not so much because of possible loss of the tax exemption Jones's church enjoyed, but because any investigation could become wider.

Parks also said she typed up "maybe fifty" applications from church members who were talked into cashing their life-insurance policies.

Another pot of gold for the church was its private printing press, a church enterprise in which Jones took particular pride and interest. Jones ordered Jeannie and Al Mills, the couple responsible for Temple publications, to study the mailings of other hard-sell preachers in the U.S.

The couple composed new layouts and color combinations almost every month as Jones copied ideas from one rival preacher or another.

Jones had Mills follow him everywhere, photographing him from every angle until the most flattering poses were found. The result of all this media-conscious homework was the satisfaction of being the best-looking miracle worker on paper, to Jones's mind. But for the Millses the results showed in other ways.

"As a result of these mailings we averaged about $800 per day [during the early 1970s], and that is a very conservative figure," she said.

The publication effort spilled into another church sideline. Photographs of Jones, encased in plastic envelopes, were peddled to members who believed the image of Father was a talisman to ward off burglars, illness, and traffic accidents.

Birdie Marable sold nine different Jones pictures from a tray that she carried like a nightclub cigarette girl during weekend services. "I made $80 to $100 a meeting" she said.

Such routine methods were the steadiest producers but the church accrued larger sums through property transfers.

Between 1967 and 1977, the church or its officials were involved in thirty-two recorded real estate transactions. Ten of these were gifts of property to the church by Temple members. In San Francisco in 1977 the church sold two pieces of property: a three-unit apartment at 1660–64 Page Street for $127,000 on June 21 and a pair of flats at 258 Howth Street for $42,500 on May 12.

In addition there were sales in which Temple officials used the power of attorney signed over by members. For example, a rest home owned by James and Irene Edwards at 2704–8 21st Street was sold on July 1, 1977, for $90,000.

The Edwards couple had left San Francisco in early 1977 for Guyana. They departed on short notice, leaving the home and its furnishings, even the food in the icebox to be taken care of by church leaders. Temple secretary Jean F. Brown had power of attorney and signed sale documents prepared by Temple lawyer Gene Chaikin.

But the average Temple member was never in a position to offer the church such wealth, former members pointed out. The vast majority were people like Jessie Boyd, an elderly black widow who lived alone in a one-room studio apartment run by the San Francisco Housing Authority in the Tenderloin ghetto.

She paid a quarter of her monthly income of $403 in rent and, until she left in February of this year, she paid another quarter to the church. In her 6½ years as a Temple member, she signed over to the church checks totaling $3937.19. These checks were deposited in four church bank accounts: the Bank of Upper Lake, the Bank of America, and Wells Fargo, all in Ukiah near Redwood Valley, and the Bank of Montreal, a San Francisco branch of a Canadian bank with offices in Georgetown, the capital of Guyana.

Mrs. Boyd also baked seven or eight cakes every week. "I bought all the fixings myself, and the church would take it over to the Safeway or Albertson's and sell each one for five dollars.

"I can't tell you how much I may have given in little bits of cash," she said.

But still, whether the money sat spilling out of bank sacks in the Temple office or stored neatly in bank accounts, there was a lot of it to spend. The church pegged its yearly budget around $600,000. There was much more money on hand, though, former members agreed. Most of it was squirreled away in bank accounts in Panama and Europe. In late 1973 another destination for the Temple's money emerged: its newly founded colony in the jungle outback of Guyana.

Carving out a community in the remote Guyana countryside was an expensive proposition. Jones himself once announced to the church it was costing $1 million per year. But he was apparently too nervous about money to trust shifting it through official channels, preferring to send trusted couriers with as much as $50,000 in cash by plane from San Francisco to Georgetown.

Dan Phillips, who went with Jones and about a dozen top church leaders to Guyana on the Temple's first visit in December 1973, said a large sum was transferred then.

"Each of us had $5000 in cash. There was also a bank draft for $600,000 from Barclay's of Canada to deposit in the bank's branch in Georgetown."

With all these revelations, with all the witnesses testifying to fraud, indignity, and punishment, the world outside the Temple rarely noticed and certainly never cried out.

Occasionally, in California newspapers, a disaffected Temple member would speak out about the abuses being perpetrated by Jones, but few in the media ever saw any pattern or reason to force a public inquiry. Even when Jones was arrested in Los Angeles for making lewd advances to an undercover policeman the charges were quickly dropped—and the arrest record has been destroyed. The arrest at the time was so obscure—who had ever heard of a man named Jones?—that not a paragraph appeared in print.

It wasn't until July 1977, after Jones had abandoned San Francisco to his Temple subordinates to lead his cult at its jungle outpost in Jonestown, that District Attorney Joseph Freitas of San Francisco opened an official investigation.

But Freitas did not announce his inquiry, nor did he disclose its negative results until after the Jonestown massacre. Only then did he feel impelled to release the report—apparently in order to counter charges that he had never probed the Temple at all.

In fact, Freitas had assigned five investigators from his special prosecutions team to examine all the charges current against Jones and the Temple leadership. The confidential report noted that charges had been raised of homicide, child abduction, extortion, arson, battery, illegal drug use, diversion of welfare funds, and kidnapping. But the investigators insisted, after taking testimony from seventy witnesses, that they could not confirm a single charge, or develop enough evidence to sustain a single prosecution.

The final report to the district attorney placed the Peoples Temple inquiry on "inactive status," although the investigators did agree that the Temple leadership's practices were "at least unsavory" and raised "substantial" moral questions.

With that report still buried in the files, there was little for the press to follow. At times reporters would poke around the Temple in San Francisco, attending services there under the watchful eyes of Temple members. An *Examiner* reporter tried to get permission from Jones to visit the Guyana settlement, but the answer was no. Another *Examiner* reporter was invited by Jones, but didn't go. Kilduff asked the *Chronicle*'s editors to approve a trip to Jonestown, and was told he might go if he was certain he could have free and unlimited access to all the people there, and that Jones would stand by such a guarantee. The project never passed the talking stage.

7

GUYANA

The republic of Guyana (formerly British Guiana) is a densely forested, Minnesota-sized nation perched on the eastern shoulder of South America. The name is derived from the Amerindian term *guiana*, "land of waters," which was applied to the entire Amazon watershed region. The former colony became independent in 1966, and the socialist government has since then been engaged in efforts to diversify the country's sugar-based plantation economy. The native Amerindians make up only 5 percent of the population of around 1 million; East Indians brought in by the British as indentured workers constitute the single largest ethinic group, followed by the descendants of African slaves. Situated not far north of the equator, Guyana has two rainy seasons when the rivers flood: February and August. The average temperature is a humid 75°–80°F.

Wildlife abounds, including the giant anteater, the sloth, and the cayman, a relative of the alligator. Some parts of the low-lying interior remain virtually unexplored, except by the aboriginal Amerindians.

More than 33 percent of the population is Hindu, about 40 percent Christian, and 9 percent Muslim.

When Jim Jones first visited Guyana in the 1960s he fell in love with the Victorian houses, and he thought the people were sweet and friendly. He also believed the Guyanese people were receptive to his brand of "spiritual healing."

There were other reasons Jones liked Guyana. The official and principal language was English. A large proportion of the population was black (as was the majority of the Peoples Temple congregation). Transportation was not too costly as the country was relatively close to the United States.

The politics of Guyana also attracted Jones. The young government espoused a socialist, though not a Marxist, line. And the country was poor, very poor. That meant it would be cheap to live in.

"Jim thought about Canada, but he said it was too bourgeois," an aide reported. "And he said in Africa a bloody black-white confrontation was coming."

On December 9, 1973, the first four emissaries from Peoples Temple, all members of Jones's inner circle, landed in the capital city of Georgetown, each carrying nearly $5000. They rented a house and a Volkswagen and set up a series of appointments with government officials. On December 16, another twelve Temple members went to Guyana. Their mission was to find out more about Guyanese society, and to find a site for the planned "agricultural mission."

Jones had set two criteria for the location of the settlement: it had to be isolated, and there had to be a reasonable possibility of improving the land. The fact-finding group decided the northwest region of the country looked best. There was plenty of accessible fresh water the land seemed to hold potential and the area was largely uninhabited, except for scattered Amerindian villages. The area was also close to Venezuela so that if the settlers ever had to escape the country they wouldn't have far to flee. The Guyanese government encouraged the choice, because in its long-standing border dispute with Venezuela it would be aided by the presence of an active, thriving settlement.

Jones himself went down to oversee the final choice. In a government-provided twenty-seat plane Jones and his lieutenants toured the jungle, focusing on an area near the towns of Port Kaituma and Matthews Ridge in the far northwest corner.

Jones's first choice, a site near Matthews Ridge was disallowed by the government. He was finally allowed to lease—for the reported sum of $200–$300 a year—a 27,000-acre parcel some thirty miles from the first selection and about six miles from Port Kaituma, a sleepy river town.

Jones returned to San Francisco and was ecstatic. He immediately created a new church department to oversee the development of what he told his flock was the "promised land."

Guyana was never the paradise Jim Jones claimed. From the beginning, Temple members had problems, most of them resulting from miscalculations by the zealous but unschooled band of frontiersmen. Early settlers at Jonestown faced a hot, steamy climate teeming with poisonous snakes, and a wily local population of Amerindians who delighted in pilfering the curious newcomers' stores. The settlers plowed the furrows for their first crops uphill and down, so that the first rains washed away precious topsoil. The indigenous purpleheart and greenheart trees were of such hard wood that the pilgrims ruined several saws trying to clear them, and in the middle of some of the densest forest on earth they were forced to import their lumber from the town of Matthews Ridge, thirty miles away. The growing settlement attracted a growing multitude of rats. The first crude buildings included earthen floors and tin roofs but no walls, so that at night the weary newcomers slept under crude canopies of mosquito netting that deterred only some of the insects.

But Jonestown, Guyana, was where Jim Jones wanted to establish his refuge against the holocaust, whether nuclear destruction or race war. So Jonestown it was.

In November 1974 Jones took a large delegation of fifty church members from San Francisco to Guyana on a chartered turboprop plane routed through Mexico. Jones wanted to impress his new countrymen with a faith healing.

He asked Timothy Stoen to fake a stomach ailment at a church service in Georgetown with Guyanese officials and journalists in attendance.

"I had to fake it through the whole meeting," Stoen said. "I never was much good at that." Jones "cured" the patient, of course, but the stunt he had designed to curry favor with his hosts backfired.

"The journalists there were very sharp and got onto the healing thing right away. They gave us a lot of bad publicity." Stoen said Jones asked the government to put a halt to the bad press, but officials refused.

"It was a major blunder and it made me doubt him for the first time," said Stoen.

Undeterred Jones decided to fake a photograph to illustrate the Guyanese paradise his sermons described. Jones aides went to a Georgetown grocery store and bought bananas, grapefruit, and oranges and arranged them around Jones, who knelt before sapling orange trees to make them look taller. The resulting photograph made the settlement look like a cornucopia, an Eden.

By the beginning of 1975 there were fifteen Temple members at Jonestown full-time, clearing land and erecting the first structures with the help of a hired Amerindian crew. By December 1976, when California's Lieutenant Governor Mervyn Dymally dropped in at Jonestown on his way home from a vacation in Trinidad, fifty people lived at the settlement.

Gradually the Jonestown settlers began to make headway in taming the jungle. "In the early days there was a holiday spirit," Stoen said. "We had touch football games in the hour before dinner. It was like Bobby Kennedy's family."

Around the same time the Temple purchased for $50,000 a five-bedroom house in the exclusive Lamaha Gardens district of Georgetown. It became the church's headquarters in the capital.

In the settlement's early days Jones became cozy with the government of Prime Minister Forbes Burnham, and especially Deputy Prime Minister Ptolemy Reid, with whom Jones had a series of meetings. Eventually the Guyanese government was accused by local critics of looking the other way when the Jonestown commune, using its three boats, shipped out produce and brought in supplies without going through a customs check. There were reports that Jones and his followers helped Burnham in at least one political campaign.

"But we never really investigated them," said an editor of the leading opposition newspaper. "There were lots of charges and suspicions, but at the same time I received numerous letters from friends in the United States telling me what a wonderful group it was."

In May 1977 there were still only about seventy full-time residents at the Jonestown mission. Jones himself was spending most of his time in San Francisco. But then came a series of critical newspaper and magazine articles—including the articles in *New West*—which Peoples Temple publications denounced as a CIA-FBI-Interpol-media conspiracy to destroy the

INSIDE THE SUICIDE CULT

Rev. Jim Jones in March, 1976.
STEPHANIE MAZE SAN FRANCISCO CHRONICLE

The Peoples Temple on Geary Street in San Francisco.
JOHN STOREY SAN FRANCISCO CHRONICLE

Rev. Jim Jones (holding sign) in 1976,
leading a demonstration
for four jailed Fresno newsmen.
WIDE WORLD PHOTOS

If it were for me
to choose between
the government
without the press
or the press with-
out government,
I should not hesitate
to choose the latter."
—Thomas Jefferson

From left, Rev. Jim Jones, Eric Gary, Prime Minister of Grenada, and Calif. Lt. Gov. Mervyn Dymally with two unidentified men at San Francisco Peoples Temple karate demonstration.
SUSAN EHMER SAN FRANCISCO CHRONICLE

Rep. Leo J. Ryan
in 1970 investigating
prison conditions
at Folsom Prison.
WIDE WORLD PHOTOS

Charles Garry, Peoples Temple lawyer,
Nov. 14, 1978, just
before he left for Jonestown.
SUSAN EHMER SAN FRANCISCO CHRONICLE

Mark Lane, one of the Peoples Temple lawyers.
JOHN O'HARA SAN FRANCISCO CHRONICLE

Rep. Leo J. Ryan (D.–Calif.).
SUSAN EHMER SAN FRANCISCO CHRONICLE

Marceline Jones, who died with her husband in Guyana.
JOHN O'HARA SAN FRANCISCO CHRONICLE

Aerial view of some of the dead at Jonestown, Nov. 21, 1978. UPI

A Guyanese man, standing beside a dead dog, inspects bodies of fallen Temple members, on Nov. 20, 1978.

Some of the weapons found in Jonestown, Guyana. UPI

Confiscated passports of sect members
found after the mass suicide. WIDE WORLD PHOTOS

PASSPORT
PASSPORT

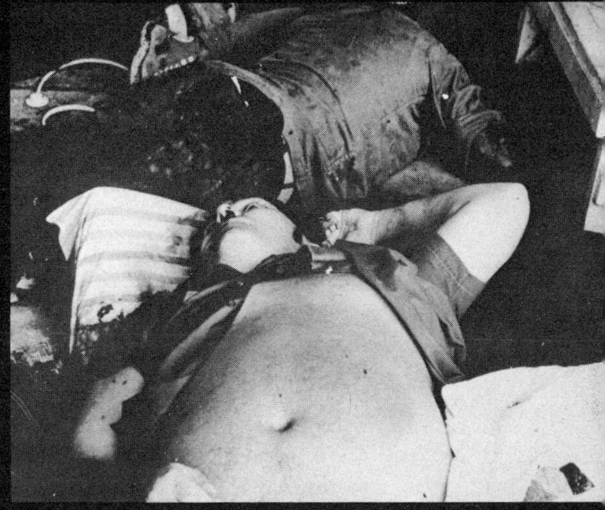

The body of Rev. Jim Jones. UPI

The vat containing the cyanide-laced Kool-Aid. UPI

Shelby Bird (right), whose aunt and uncle were in Jonestown, is comforted by Bishop Paul Miles at the Peoples Temple in San Francisco.
JOHN STOREY SAN FRANCISCO CHRONICLE

Michael Prokes (center) and Tim Carter (right) members of the Peoples Temple cult, in custody of Guyanese troops.
WIDE WORLD PHOTOS

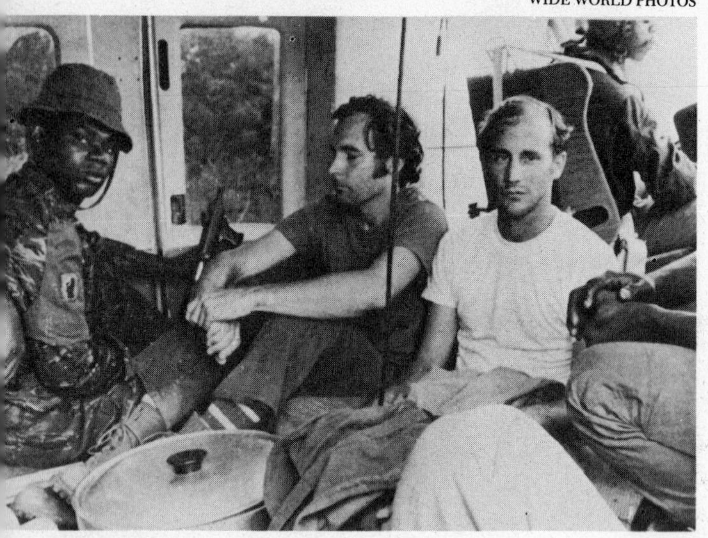

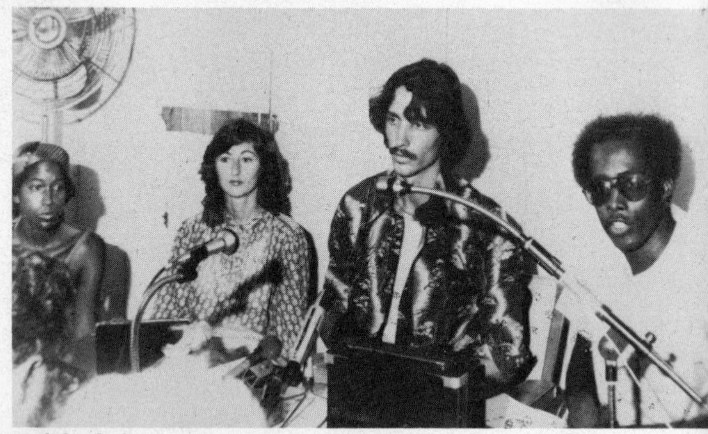

Cult leader's son, Stephan Jones (center) denounces his father at a press conference. He escaped the "white night" of destruction because he was in a basketball tournament in Georgetown, Guyana. UPI

Lena Pietila, a former sect member, reflects on the news from Guyana.
SUSAN EHMER SAN FRANCISCO CHRONICLE

Margie Henderson (left), whose mother was in Guyana, tries to get past a guard at Peoples Temple in San Francisco.
JOHN STOREY SAN FRANCISCO CHRONICLE

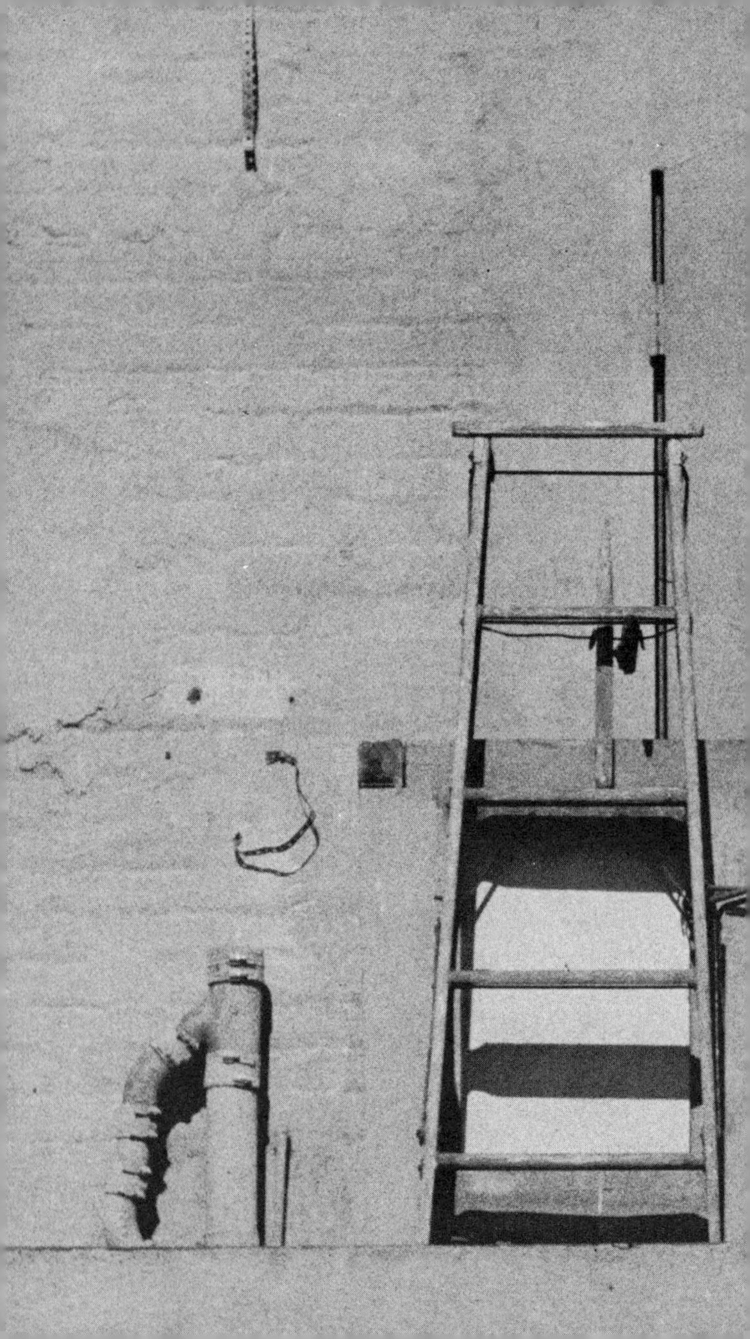

In San Francisco, Temple members watch and wait following the news from Guyana.
JOHN STOREY SAN FRANCISCO CHRONICLE

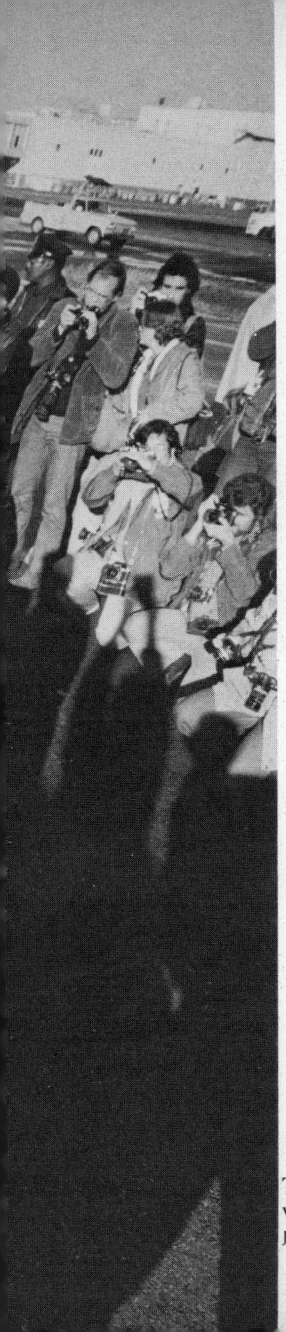

The Ryan family
watches his hearse.
JOHN STOREY SAN FRANCISCO CHRONICLE

Rep. Ryan's casket arrives in San Francisco.
JOHN STOREY SAN FRANCISCO CHRONICLE

church. Jones's paranoia increased until finally he decided it was time to leave the United States. By the end of 1977 Jones and the bulk of the congregation had left for Guyana, leaving behind only a hundred people to send supplies. Temple members who made the trip signed away to the church their cars, homes, possessions—at Jonestown, there would be no need for the trappings of their former lives.

Rosemary Williams was one of the Temple members who made the trip. Williams, who works at a San Francisco bank, and her husband Harry, a city plumber, called their children one morning to tell them they would be leaving on a trip immediately, and to select their favorite possessions. The Williamses refused to tell their children where they were going or how long they would be gone.

"I was crying and asking mom to tell me what was going on," said the Williams' daughter Unjolla Daniels. "She had a cold nature to her, she didn't seem to hear us. Why, all her life she had been one of the most emotional people I knew—she used to cry or grow sad all the time." Rosemary Williams said later she and her husband had been acting on Jones's orders.

The couple, along with several family members and friends, piled into a station wagon and drove straight through to Miami without stopping. Their daughter Yolanda, who made the motor trip but was not a church member, tried to keep them from going on to Guyana and succeeded in delaying them for a month. Harry Williams finally decided to drive back to San

Francisco because quitting his job would mean losing his city pension. But Rosemary Williams decided to go on to Guyana.

She had joined the church in 1970, when it was still located in Redwood Valley. She had recently undergone exploratory surgery for cancer, and doctors had found nothing, but she had remained disturbed. At a church service Jones "cured" her of cancer once and for all, and produced a chunk of flesh—supposedly the tumor—as proof. From then on she did everything Jones told her to do, until she spent a week in Jonestown. She was allowed to leave, and she came back to San Francisco with a succinct evaluation of Jim Jones's paradise: "It is natural hell."

Discipline at the camp was strict, Rosemary Williams said, even for youngsters. If a child wet his bed, she reported, he was given electric shocks. If a child defecated in his pants, he was forced to wear his underwear on his head.

One youth, sixteen-year-old Tommy Bogue, was forced to dig a latrine from 10:00 p.m. to 6:00 a.m. because supervisors discovered he had stolen some aluminum roofing sheets to make a small hut for himself outside the main settlement area. Other youngsters were forced to eat hot peppers for violating Jones's rules.

For the older Temple members life at Jonestown had much in common with the strict regimen they had followed in California. According to one witness, after a workday that for some began at 6:00 a.m. and ended at 10:00 p.m., there might be a four-hour "catharsis" session during which individuals would be ridiculed for doubting the progress of the mission or failing in their assignments. A rule breaker might have his head shaved or be forced to wear a yellow hard hat as a badge of dishonor or told not to speak for several days. If clothing or tools were damaged or lost, the offender was fined the replacement cost. Since no one had any money, the member would be denied his meals—which the church computed as costing one dollar each—until the debt was repaid.

Like other Temple members who made the trip, Williams entered the country at Georgetown, staying at the residence there. Members in the capital city were expected to beg food from Georgetown shopkeepers using the ruse that donations would be sent to Jonestown. In fact, the food went to support the Georgetown group, and only a small portion made its way to Jonestown.

The trip from Georgetown to the jungle settlement was by either plane or boat. The 150-mile plane trip to the Port Kaituma airstrip took one hour. A church truck transported the travelers the additional eight miles to the mission. By sea the trip took twenty-three hours. The boat ran up the Kaituma River, past tiny Amerindian villages dotted between the awesome foliage of the tropical rain forest. As soon as Temple members arrived, the church confiscated their money and passports.

Meanwhile, church members who remained in San Francisco busied themselves sending supplies and equipment to the outpost. They communicated with Jonestown by shortwave radio, and other ham radio operators became incensed at the way the Temple violated Federal Communications Commission regulations. Church members used amateur radio frequencies to transact business, which is illegal, and often spoke in code, also prohibited.

Jones's code name was "Al"—no action could be taken in San Francisco or Jonestown until "Al" gave his approval. Reporter Marshall Kilduff became "Morris." Other reporters were known as "philosophers." The names of chess pieces were also used in the church's radio code, which was changed frequently.

Ham radio operators reported that the Temple members treated the frequencies they used as private property, and refused to allow access to anyone else. The FCC monitored church broadcasts for nearly a year, and eventually fined one of the Temple operators $50 for failing to give adequate station identification.

Jones himself shuttled back and forth between the colony and Georgetown, dealing with government officials and supervising the arrival of followers from California. The church made no official announcement of the exodus, and relatives of those who had gone to Guyana without leaving word were faced with a stone wall of silence when they made inquiries at the San Francisco Temple. Some families complained to the San Francisco district attorney, and his office found that by mid-August 1977 nearly 400 Peoples Temple members had left for Jonestown.

Rosemary Williams hated the place and

wanted to leave almost as soon as she arrived. She hated the discipline—she was put to work in the kitchen. She found the food adequate, but the housing—one-room shacks bulging with people and two large dormitories—intolerable. There was no hot water, and newsprint was used as toilet paper. Williams said she lost ten pounds in the four days she worked at Jonestown. She went back to Georgetown and told Jones that she wanted to leave.

"He told me I would have a stroke and all sorts of baloney," she said, "but I told him I wanted to go home." She said Temple members let her place a phone call to her brother in San Francisco, but stood beside her while she talked and recorded the conversation.

Finally she was allowed to leave. But she had to promise she would never speak of her dislike for Jonestown, and would say instead that she was returning home so she could continue to work toward a pension. Peoples Temple publications continued to laud the settlement as a model community. In newsletters and its own newspaper, the Temple emphasized the modern medical equipment, the educational program, the incipient herd of cattle, and the unfinished sawmill.

"The excellent health of residents here and the astounding growth of the project are glowing and reflections of the spirit of socialist cooperations," reported a newsletter. "The experience of Jonestown, and the inspiration of its founder-leader Jim Jones is building healthy and happy lives. We are more proud than we can say of what we have been able to accomplish in such a short time in this beautiful jungle interior."

Perhaps the most glowing praise of all came from Peoples Temple attorney Charles Garry after a 1977 visit, whose words appeared in *Peoples Forum,* the Temple newspaper:

"From what I saw there, I would say that the society that is being built in Jonestown is a credit to humanity.

"I have seen paradise."

8

JONESTOWN: THE BEGINNING OF THE END

The Peoples Temple exodus from San Francisco was veiled in the kind of secrecy that observers had come to expect from the church. Often, departing members were called in the morning and told they would leave for Guyana the same night. The church stated it would continue to keep its home base in San Francisco, but the Geary Boulevard Temple became little more than a supply depot for the jungle settlement. "We are absolutely not pulling out of San Francisco or California," a church press release stated, denouncing news accounts of the hegira as "biased and sensationalistic reporting."

But the Temple was unable to plug all the leaks, and accounts of mysterious departures by church members slowly emerged. LaFlora Townes, a church member and a chambermaid for fifteen years at San Francisco's Carlton Hotel, phoned her employer late one night and said she had to leave town immediately. Another woman, a nurse, said she had to leave town "to take care of business back east." Her employer said she was a member of the church. The local district attorney's office confirmed in August 1977 that between twenty and forty members of the church, who had all been living in an apartment near the Temple, had left suddenly for Jonestown. Several families complained to the D.A. that relatives were missing and believed to be in Guyana, but investigators were unable to discover the relatives' whereabouts. Larry Tupper said he had been awarded legal custody of his son Larry, Jr., but charged that the boy was in Guyana with his mother, who was a member of the church. Neva Sly, who left the church, alleged that her son Mark, sixteen, was sent to Guyana against his will. The guardian of young Vincent Lopez heard rumors of brainwashing, mind control, and beatings at Jonestown, and asked that the boy be returned.

Persons who tried to investigate the goings-on at Jonestown were greeted with the same tactics of obfuscation as were members' families. Freelance writer Kathy Hunter, wife of *Ukiah Daily Journal* Executive Editor George Hunter, went to Guyana after receiving what she believed was an invitation for the visit from Guyana Prime Minister Forbes Burnham. Hunter had met Burnham several years before when he made a visit to the northern California town.

"I went with an open mind, I really did," she said. "I have always been a friend of Jim Jones, and I didn't really believe some of the things they said about him. But now I can only believe he's not the same man that I knew."

Hunter said that on her arrival in the Guyanese capital she was told the invitation was a hoax. Meanwhile, she said, she was harassed by "a squad of interrogators" from the jungle settlement, who shadowed her at her Georgetown hotel and bugged her telephone.

For seven of the nine days Hunter spent in Guyana, she was confined to her hotel room in "protective custody" by the authorities, she said. She finally returned to the United States shaken but unharmed—and she had never made it to Jonestown.

An even more chilling report came from Jeff Haas, a San Francisco attorney. Hass represented Grace Stoen, former Temple lieutenant Tim Stoen's wife, in a custody battle with Jim Jones over the Stoen's six-year-old son, John Victor. Jones claimed the Stoens agreed to have him sire the boy, and once said the main reason he would never return to the United States was that he might be forced to surrender custody of the child. By September 1977 both the Stoens had left the church and Grace Stoen wanted her son back. So Haas went to Guyana.

"We had a court order from here in California compelling Jones to surrender custody of Grace's boy," Haas said. He said he had hoped his arrival would surprise Jones, but State Department officials had already informed church members that Haas was on his way.

Haas arrived in Georgetown. "We had hoped the Guyanese officials would simply recognize the California court order and enforce it, but they said they couldn't do that." This meant Haas would have to fight for custody of the child in Guyanese courts. On Grace Stoen's behalf he retained a local attorney, Clarence Hughes. The first step was to serve Jones with papers ordering him to bring the child to court.

"I had to hire a plane to Jonestown so we could serve the papers," Haas said. Haas flew to the outpost and tried to serve Jones with the court summons.

"When we got there we asked for Jones, but Maria Katsaris [Jones's mistress] intervened. She said Jones hadn't been there for two days." Haas said he and his party stayed at Jonestown only about thirty minutes and saw no sign of the leader. He asked to be allowed to wander around the compound, but was refused permission.

But Haas said that on the way back to the airstrip from Jonestown, his party overtook two Guyanese immigration officials, who had been to the settlement and talked to Jones only forty-five minutes earlier. Haas thought better of going back to Jonestown for a confrontation, deciding instead to return to Georgetown and the next stage of the court battle.

He and Hughes received permission from the Guyanese court to waive a requirement that Jones personally receive the summons. Several days later, he and Tony London, a Guyanese law enforcement official for the Jonestown area, returned to the camp to post notices informing Jones that he had to bring the boy to court. "This time," he said, "the people were very hostile."

As fast as Haas and London could post the court notices, church members tore them down, he said. "They said they would not accept the summons, on the advice of their attorney." Once again, Jones was nowhere to be found.

"While we were talking to them a bunch of young boys gathered around us. It was a threatening situation, but there was nothing overt."

Haas said Temple members told London, whose position was roughly that of an under-sheriff, that three days earlier two men had tried to assassinate Jones at Jonestown—the same day Haas had been told that Jones was not there.

Haas said London pointed out the discrepancy, and the Temple members replied that the attempted assassination "must have happened the day before." But London reminded church members that they had told Haas they hadn't seen Jones for two days before the attorney's first visit.

"Then things got a little heated," Haas said "Tony London asked me to go sit in our jeep while he investigated the purported assassination attempt." While he was waiting, Haas said, a man came walking down the road carrying a 12-gauge shotgun.

"At that point, I didn't know what the hell was happening," Haas said. "I jumped out and dove behind the jeep."

It turned out, the attorney said, that London had asked to see all the guns in the camp. The settlers had brought him two—the shotgun and a pistol.

On this visit, Haas spent about forty-five minutes at Jonestown. Again, he was not allowed to roam unescorted, though he did get to see the central pavilion area. "There was no physical confrontation, but the situation was certainly emotionally charged," he said. He was frightened.

"We went back to Georgetown, where the court process just stopped," Haas related. "We tried to get an arrest warrant for Jones, but the court clerk refused to sign it, and he was the only one who could. We heard that there was interference by government officials." Haas succeeded in getting an American consular official to write a letter to the government complaining of the court's glacial pace. But Jonestown responded with an affidavit accusing Grace Stoen of being an unfit mother.

Haas came home. A hearing on the case was set for January 1978. Haas went back to Georgetown, along with Grace and Tim Stoen. But the judge sitting on the case said his life had been threatened because of the case and disqualified himself, and the case had to begin again with a new judge. While in Guyana, the Stoens say, they were threatened with death by Temple members if they did not drop the proceedings. They were never allowed to see their son.

Steven A. Katsaris, a Mendocino County psychologist, who directs a treatment center for children with severe behavior problems, struggled for months to get to see his daughter Maria, who lived in Jones's cabin at Jonestown and was the leader's mistress. When he finally succeeded, she was a changed woman.

According to an affidavit signed by Katsaris, his twenty-five-year-old daughter told him in

July 1977 that she was leaving San Francisco for Jonestown. She said she would be there only for a few weeks, but later tlephoned to say she would stay several weeks longer. Around the same time, Katsaris read newspaper accounts of "psychological and physical coercion" at Jonestown, and became concerned. His daughter told him by phone not to worry, that she was fine. Katsaris told Maria he wanted to visit Jonestown, and she "appeared enthusiastic and receptive to this idea," the psychologist said.

Maria sent her father letters that brimmed with her enthusiasm for Jonestown. "Coming down the Kaituma River is one of my most favorite things," she wrote in one. "It is hard to describe how beautiful it is. It is so peaceful. I like to sit out on the deck and watch all the scenery, all the animals and birds plus all the different kinds of tropical plants." She wrote extensively about the food the settlers ate at Jonestown, and especially liked a strain of beans they cultivated called the cutlass bean. "They came up with a way to fix it so it tastes just like sausage patties," Maria Katsaris wrote her father. "I wouldn't care if I never ate meat again if I had my cutlass patties."

"One last thing," she wrote. "Please, please, please do not get disturbed by the bad publicity the church has gotten. It is absolutely incredible that the press can print such a filthy bunch of lies and are allowed to get by with it . . . I am not surprised though. A society that is based on economic inequality and classism is certainly not going to let an organization advocating economic and racial equality exist too easily. But no matter what they think, they will not succeed."

The letter ended: "I love you and miss you. So write. Your daughter, Maria."

Katsaris arranged to arrive in Guyana on September 26, 1977, and called church offices in San Francisco to have them relay his time of arrival to Maria. For several nights thereafter, his affidavit said, he received phone calls warning him not to make the trip. One caller warned that Katsaris's home was in an isolated area and could easily be burned down.

On September 14, Maria called. She asked that Katsaris delay his trip until December, when a group of clergy would be visiting Jonestown. "The radiophone call was prolonged with many pauses and interruptions but the essence of the conversation was a series of obstacles presented to me by my daughter to discourage me from visiting," Katsaris wrote. Maria said church policy was not to permit visitors. Katsaris pointed out that Maria's letters indicated there were visitors at Jonestown almost daily. He reminded his daughter that he had supported her work with the church, and asked if he could meet her in Georgetown. After a pause, Maria told him she would be in Venezuela at the time of the intended visit. Katsaris suggested meeting Maria in Venezuela, but she claimed she would be there with her "fiancé," Larry Schacht, the Jonestown medical officer. Katsaris said he subsequently learned that other parents had been told their daughters were engaged or married to Schacht, apparently in an attempt by the

Temple to assure the parents that their children were about to be married to professionals.

"The long pauses in the conversation made me suspect she was being coached," Katsaris wrote in the affidavit. "When I finally told her that I was upset and frightened and that I would use every legal and diplomatic means to see her, she replied that she would not see me even if I did come to Guyana."

The following day, Katsaris sent a telegram to Jim Jones telling of his concern for his daughter. Jones never replied.

When Katsaris arrived in Guyana he was greeted at the American embassy in Georgetown with a declaration signed by Maria that she did not want to see her father. According to Katsaris, a Temple representative, Paula Adams, had told American officials that he was a child molester who had sexually abused his daughter. Confused and dejected, Katsaris went home.

Katsaris interviewed as many former members of the Temple as he could find, and discovered that his daughter was a member of the inner circle of the church. He also learned that she had been required to sign an undated suicide note that could be used to explain her disappearance if she ever left the church.

"I lived in constant anxiety for my daughter's safety," Katsaris wrote. "I was convinced that Peoples Temple Church was using their humanitarian efforts and social welfare activities to cover for their ultimate goal which is the establishment of world socialism (fascism?) with Jim Jones as their leader, and that they would stop at nothing including calumny, character assassination, blackmail, threats of violence and even murder to achieve their goal."

In November Katsaris returned to Georgetown and finally had his meeting with Maria. "She looked as if she had not slept well or [as if she] had been deprived of sleep over a long period of time and her general attitude was one of suspicion, hostility and paranoia," Katsaris wrote. "The entire meeting was extremely painful for me and depressing. I managed to tell my daughter that if she ever wanted to return home a ticket would be waiting for her at the embassy. When I told her of my belief in God and that somehow things would work out, she and another woman from the church were quick to point out to me that they do not believe in God."

Katsaris made no further attempts to reach Maria for fear that doing so would jeopardize her life. He did, however, join a group of parents and relatives of Temple members in pushing for an investigation of the church, and helped persuade Congressman Leo Ryan to make his trip to Jonestown.

He and the other relatives were particularly disturbed by a letter Jim Jones sent to each U.S. senator and congressman in March 1978.

"We at Peoples Temple have been the subject of harassment by several agencies of the U.S. government and are rapidly reaching the point at which our patience is exhausted," the letter began, and went on to describe a "conspiracy" against Jones and his followers. But the end of the letter was what sent chills up Katsaris's spine:

"I can say without hesitation that we are devoted to a decision that it is better even to die than to be constantly harassed from one continent to the next."

9

DEBORAH LAYTON: ESCAPE AND REVELATIONS

In 1971 Deborah Layton was eighteen and just another young face on the streets and sidewalks of Berkeley. But she was not one of the rootless street people. She had grown up there, as the pretty, brown-haired daughter of an affluent family—a family whose membership in Peoples Temple eventually included her mother and her older brother, Larry.

Her early trips to the services at Peoples Temple profoundly affected her. She wanted to be part of this effort to help others. The strong sense of mission and discipline was a great contrast to the aimless, drug-oriented ferment in Berkeley. And it was that serious sense of purpose that won this attractive, thoughtful young girl over to Jim Jones.

Jones and his lieutenants showed tremendous, and flattering, respect for her competence despite her youth. She became financial secretary of the Peoples Temple and a confidant of Jones.

As the financial secretary, Layton knew the temple in San Francisco received and cashed at least $65,000 in social security checks each month. Little of the money went to the elderly members of the church. Most went to the "reserve" fund, the rest to help set up the experimental community in Guyana.

When she got to Jonestown in 1977, Layton already knew something of the way Jones operated.

"During the years I was a member . . . I watched the organization depart with increasing frequency from its professed dedication to social change and democracy."

Jones, she said, "gradually assumed a tyrannical hold over the lives of Temple members."

Debbi Layton enjoyed watching and listening to Jones preach in the San Francisco Temple headquarters. Most of the time she felt he didn't make sense. What preacher who talks for three or four hours at a stretch does? But, she said, "When I first joined the Temple, Reverend Jones seemed to make a clear distinction between fantasy and reality . . . most of the times when he said irrational things, he was aware that they were irrational but that they served as tools of his leadership.

"His theory was that the end justified the means."

For those, like Layton, who believed in Jones's vision of the future, watching him perform was exciting. He played on a listener's emotions, alternately praising and threatening, making evil threats, then describing the safety to be gained by faith in him and his interpretation of the gospels.

Jones's own faith in Deborah Layton was underscored shortly before her arrival in Jonestown. He trusted her to monitor radio broadcasts in San Francisco from the busy jungle commune. The messages to California became more and more bizarre.

Jones said he was under attack. Former Temple member Grace Stoen had just sent her attorney, Jeff Haas, to Guyana in the complicated child custody case involving her son. Jones's tirades against Grace and her husband went on and on, over the radio, in public and during Temple services.

Then the radio crackled with an assignment for Layton and several other California members of the Temple: find Timothy Stoen. Bribe him to stop attacking Jones's good work.

If $5000 wouldn't do it, offer as much as $10,000.

Stoen could not be bribed, however. So other instructions came from Jonestown: Meet Stoen in San Francisco Superior Court, ambush him in the hall, and by threat intimidate him from going inside. Again, the mission failed.

By late fall 1977 the radio messages from Guyana became even more frenzied and hysterical.

Jones's public relations adviser in San Francisco was Terry J. Buford. She and Layton were instructed to deliver a message to officials of the government of Guyana.

The message was extraordinary: Unless the

government of Guyana took immediate steps to stall the Guyanese court action on John Victor Stoen's custody, the entire population of Jonestown would extinguish itself in a mass suicide by 5:30 p.m. that day.

Layton and Buford could not reach Guyanese officials by telephone. But they knew other Temple members were given the same task.

A short time later a new message arrived by radio. Mission successful. The court case had been stalled, the suicide threat called off.

When Layton arrived in Jonestown, she soon realized that the mass suicide threat delivered to the Guyanese government was not an empty one.

For one thing, there were the loudspeakers.

The loudspeakers in Jonestown repeated the Jones messages over and over. Jones was on the air an average of six hours per day. He ranted about "traitors" who left the Temple. And he talked of the punishment for treason—death. When especially agitated, he went on seemingly forever, nonstop. At times he claimed he was the reincarnation of Lenin, Jesus Christ, or other historical and religious figures. He had powerful friends the world over, he said, ranging from the leaders of the Soviet Union to Idi Amin (the mad dictator of Uganda).

On and on the loudspeakers blared. Even if a commune resident was ill and could not attend the marathon camp meetings at night, he could not escape. The loudspeakers carried the words to every corner of the lonely, isolated encampment.

Later, Layton realized she had been listening

to a madman. "He claimed he had divine powers . . . that he had extrasensory perception and could heal the sick and could tell what everyone was thinking. He would not sleep for days at a time, and talked compulsively about conspiracies against him. He felt that as a consequence of being ridiculed and maligned, he would be denied a place in history. His obsession with his place in history was maniacal. When pondering the loss of what he considered his rightful place in history, he would grow despondent and say that all was lost."

The work schedule at Jonestown was grueling, just as it had been at Temple communes and properties in the United States. According to Layton, the vast majority of Temple members worked from 7:00 a.m. to 6:00 p.m. six days a week and from 7:00 a.m. to 2:00 p.m. Sundays. An hour was allotted for lunch, but most of this was spent walking back to the kitchens, standing in line, and walking back. No other rest was permitted.

Layton soon grew exhausted. She had dark circles under her eyes and experienced a severe loss of weight. Rice for breakfast, rice-water soup for lunch, and rice and beans for dinner was the diet.

Exhausted, afraid, all ties to home cut off, Debbi listened to the growing emphasis on death creep into Jones's emotional harangues.

"The concept of mass suicide for socialism arose. Because our lives were so wretched anyway, and because we were so afraid to contradict Reverend Jones, the concept was not challenged," she recalled.

The only time life brightened at Jonestown was when visitors arrived, often relatives of members, who came to inspect the jungle village. The camp literally put on a performance, with Jones the director. Workdays were shortened, music played, and people danced, the food improved.

Members of the American embassy in Georgetown came by occasionally, prompted by rumors and reports of mistreatment. They found smiling faces, devoted, fervent believers in the new beginning they were making. And, of course, all visitors heard repeated declarations of gratitude to Jim Jones.

Once a week came White Night, a chilling rehearsal for an act of unbelievable devotion to Jones. For White Night, Jones gathered the entire population together. "The situation," he said, "is hopeless." Mercenaries were in the jungle. The camp's armed guards—up to thirty men in green jungle fatigues patrolled the camp by day, about fifteen by night—would not be able to stop them. Torture awaited when the mercenaries in the jungle closed in. The only way out would be mass suicide for the glory of socialism.

Everyone was told to line up, including the children. A small glass of red liquid was given to each person. Within forty-five minutes, Jones said quietly, everyone here will be dead. Drink from the glass.

The people of Jonestown stood in the darkness, waiting to die. Families huddled close together, talking in hushed tones.

But though they drank, no one died. The convulsions did not come. Jones, happy with the performance of the camp residents, told them it was a harmless liquid they had drunk. They had passed the loyalty test. But an ominous note entered his voice as he leaned into his microphone. This night, the only armed men were the camp's own guards, he said, but the "time is not far off when it will be necessary to die."

"The physical pain of exhaustion was so great," Layton said later, "that this event was not traumatic for me."

Life became a pattern. The extraordinary discipline began to seem ordinary. Even the children accepted it. Almost anything brought punishment. For adults, a week's stay in the "box," a wooden prison 3×3×6 feet, was not unusual. For children, "Big Foot" awaited.

Ordinary childish antics and mischief resulted in a trip down a dark path, each child firmly escorted by camp enforcers, to where Jones waited at the side of a water well. White with fear, the children were hoisted and dropped by rope into the water. Other members waited in the blackness of the well, coached by Jones to seize the children and drag them underwater. In the darkness, cut off from parents and any possibility of help, the children paid for naughtiness, dunked again and again.

Later, they had to thank Daddy—the Reverend Jim Jones—loudly and repeatedly, and tell him they were sorry. If not, Big Foot would get them again. Their terrified screams often reverberated through Jonestown, then faded in the lush, silent jungle.

If the thought of escape occurred to the residents of Jonestown, it was kept secret. Layton decided to leave only when the possibility was literally thrust upon her. She did not tell her mother or brother. She simply prepared to leave.

She was assigned to Georgetown for Temple work. Once in Guyana's capital, she said later, "I became determined to escape or die trying. I surreptitiously contacted my sister, who wired me a plane ticket."

The fear and irrationality that permeated Jonestown were hard to shake. Jones told his followers he had infiltrated and put an informer in the U.S. embassy in Georgetown. Anyone, he declared, contacting the embassy to try to leave would be known to him. Debbi believed it, or half believed it. Anything seemed possible.

There was no informer, of course. Two employees at the embassy, Richard McCoy and Daniel Weber, helped Debbi get a passport and leave. It was simple. She got on a plane and left.

Layton arrived in San Francisco determined to warn the government about the strange and ominous events in Guyana. It turned out to be a difficult task. The press in San Francisco, although it had begun serious investigation of the Peoples Temple, was still moving warily. Jones had powerful friends both in government and within the newspapers. The goodwill felt toward him by large segments of the community, especially the black community, was a palpable force.

Debbi contacted attorney Jeff Haas and with him put together a detailed, sworn affidavit. In it she summarized her experience with the Temple. Its first point declared bluntly:

"The purpose of this affidavit is to call to the attention of the United States government the existence of a situation which threatens the lives of United States citizens living in Jonestown, Guyana."

The eleven-page affidavit then recounted in detail the deterioration of Jones's mental state, the content of his harangues, the armed guards in Jonestown, the near impossibility of leaving, the harsh working conditions, the inadequate diet, the terror and brutal punishment, and finally, the ritual White Night rehearsals for mass suicide.

The affidavit made the rounds of San Francisco reporters. Haas telephoned those he knew personally and asked for coverage. Most ignored him. The *San Francisco Chronicle* gave the affidavit modest coverage.

The story, published on June 16, 1978, on page 2, began:

"The Peoples Temple jungle outpost in South America was portrayed yesterday as a remote realm where the church leader, the Rev. Jim Jones, orders public beatings, maintains a squad of 50 armed guards and has involved his 1100 followers in a threat of mass suicide."

Once again, even after this story was printed, there was no widespread cry to investigate. There was only one exception—in the offices of Congressman Leo Ryan of San Mateo, California.

10

CONGRESSMAN LEO RYAN

Representative Leo Ryan, fifty-three, a Democrat from California, had been hearing reports for more than a year about beatings, secret gun caches, suicide drills, and people held against their wills at Jonestown.

He was not the first legislator to be approached by former Peoples Temple members or by anxious relatives of Jim Jones's current followers; but Ryan was the first to exhibit more than a passing interest in the Guyana situation.

Without knowing, these critics of the Peoples Temple had finally found the one man in public life who was uniquely prepared by temperament and personal interests to take a long, hard—and eventually fatal—look at the mysterious cult.

Leo Joseph Ryan, a native of Nebraska and a schoolteacher, entered politics in the mid-1950s. "Leo didn't like the way things were going during the [Senator Joseph] McCarthy era and he wanted to get into politics to do something about it," recalled Joe Holsinger, Ryan's longtime aide and best friend.

By that time, the former Midwesterner was teaching high school in the San Francisco suburb of San Bruno. He was elected in 1956, in his first try at public office, to a seat on the city council in neighboring South San Francisco, another suburb of the big city.

In 1961 Ryan took apart in an event that would eventually lead to his involvement in the Peoples Temple investigations.

Ryan was teaching English and civics at Capuchino High School in the daytime and performing his city councilman's duties at night. He was chosen to attend the inauguration of newly elected President John F. Kennedy as the faculty chaperone for the high-school band, which was to march in the inaugural parade.

Hotel accommodations were in short supply in Washington that week in January, so Ryan had to share a room with Sammy Houston, an Associated Press photographer assigned to photograph the high-school musicians from the San Francisco Bay Area. Houston's two grandchildren were one day to reach Jonestown in Guyana; no list of survivors bears their names.

Back in 1960 Houston's picture of teacher Leo Ryan and his students marching down the middle of Pennsylvania Avenue made the front pages of newspapers all over the country, and gave a shot in the arm to Ryan's fledgling political career.

The politician and the photographer remained friends through the years, and it was this relationship that would lead Ryan eventually to a rendezvous with Peoples Temple.

In the meantime, the young city councilman ran for the state assembly in 1962 and was elected to the first of five terms in the lower house of the California legislature. Ryan was the first Democrat in more than a century to represent San Mateo County in the legislature; the blue-collar and middle-class Democrat voters in the northern end of the county had finally outvoted the wealthy Republican suburbanites in the southern portion.

It didn't take Assemblyman Ryan long to establish a reputation as an aggressive, unpredictable legislator with a taste for adventure and a knack for attracting headlines.

One day he slipped quietly out of Sacramento, the state capital, and went to work as a teacher at the predominantly black Jefferson High School in a tough, poor section of south central Los Angeles. There, far from his home district, he wouldn't be recognized, and only a handful of school administrators knew that the new substitute teacher on the campus was a state legislator doing his homework on problems afflicting urban schools.

"It was a nightmare," Ryan said when he emerged from the academic underground and told his story to the newspapers.

This personal, see-it-yourself approach to lawmaking became Ryan's trademark. Some of his legislative colleagues sniffed at the San Mateo Democrat's adventures as grandstanding, but most applauded his rather ferocious aggressiveness.

"Leo believed that more legislators should go check things out, rather than take someone's word for them," Joe Holsinger explained years later. "He felt it was his duty to check out the problems of the people he represented."

In 1970 Ryan made another on-the-spot investigation by arranging to spend a week behind bars at Folsom Prison, California's maximum security institution for the most hardened convicts. It was, he said later, "the most fearful experience of my life."

Believing that one way to bring about prison reform was for public officials to see how the prison system worked from the inside, Ryan spent eight days in a 9-by-12-foot solitary confinement cell in the prison's euphemistically named adjustment center.

He let guards and inmates know of his visit beforehand and was accompanied by guards when he met with prisoners—there is a line between bravery and foolishness and Ryan never crossed it. But he did spend time with prisoners and he was driven to Folsom, handcuffed and in leg irons, in a van full of chained convicts.

Ryan's adventures generated reams of publicity. And all that helped raise him from the state assembly to the U.S. House of Representatives in 1972 as the congressman from the Eleventh District of California, a sprawling area of suburban cities and towns stretching from San Francisco halfway down the peninsula toward San Jose.

In Congress he quickly developed a reputation as a loner, a man more likely to follow his own instincts than to parrot the party line. "He was the kind of person who went off on his own," observed Representative Pete Stark, an Oakland Democrat. "There was never an assurance that just because he was a Democrat, a liberal, or from California, he would do a certain thing. Leo marched very much to his own drummer."

Ryan's see-it-for-myself attitude turned him into an inveterate traveler whose fact-finding missions carried him to nearly every continent during his years in Congress.

His political opponents liked to point out that Ryan was one of the most-traveled members of the House, but their accusations of junketeering made little dent in his comfortable reelection victories.

Ryan, twice married and divorced, was a bachelor who lived in a handsome townhouse about a mile from the Capitol in Washington. He had five children: Christopher, twenty-nine; Shannon, twenty-six; Patricia, twenty-five; Kevin, twenty-three; and Erin, twenty-one.

His rugged political individualism might have marred the career of any politician. For example, although he had been a teacher, he opposed tenure for public-school teachers and he supported experiments with voucher plans that would allow parents to send their children to private schools with public subsidies. Both stands were matters of strong personal belief, and they earned Ryan the enmity of organized teachers and other powerful union groups in his district.

Despite his frequently strained relationships

with labor, Ryan won reelection easily in 1974, 1976, and 1978—just a few days before he left for Guyana.

Ryan's constituents included the Hearst family, and he called himself "Patty Hearst's congressman" when he asked Justice Department officials to recommend commuting her sentence for participating in a San Francisco bank robbery after she was kidnapped.

His study of the Hearst case was one of Ryan's first exposures to the concept of brainwashing, a subject that would be so deeply a factor in his Peoples Temple investigations.

The stage was also set for Ryan's interest in Jim Jones's cult when, several years ago, a member of his own family became totally enmeshed in another religious cult.

"Leo saw, through his own family, the dangers involved in these cults," Holsinger recalled later. "By the time he was asked to look into Peoples Temple, he had some idea of what these groups might be doing."

The first call to investigate Peoples Temple came in spring 1977 from Ryan's old friend and brief roommate, Associated Press cameraman Sammy Houston. He wrote a letter to his congressman, and Ryan visited the Houston home in San Bruno to talk to him.

"Sammy had lost his larynx to cancer and he couldn't talk," recalls Holsinger. "So he used a slate and a piece of chalk to tell us his problem. His wife helped out too."

What Houston told Ryan was a sad story about his son, Bob, who had joined Jim Jones's flock for a while and then was killed under mysterious circumstances in an Oakland railroad yard soon after he quit the Peoples Temple. There were two beautiful little girls, Sammy Houston's granddaughters, and they were with the Jones cult in Guyana. Tears in his eyes, Houston asked his congressman to see if his granddaughters were all right and to bring them back to the United States if possible. He had heard reports, he said, of violence and sexual abuse, even of children.

Ryan was ready to take on the assignment.

Holsinger recalls: "Leo said, 'Sammy, I will do everything I can to get your grandchildren back.'"

After the Houston visit, other families began to call Ryan. Some were from his district, but many were not. They turned to the San Mateo congressman because he was the only Bay Area representative on the House International Relations Committee, and because he was the only one who seemed genuinely concerned about the problem.

Ryan tried first to work through the State and Justice departments—seeking information, and if need be, intervention. But he got nowhere. Both federal agencies insisted they were satisfied that things were peaceful at Jonestown, Holsinger later said.

By the summer of 1978 Ryan was meeting constantly with relatives of Temple members and with former Temple members. They told stories of beatings and other atrocities. Still the federal agencies declined to become involved.

The anti-Jones people urged Ryan to make a personal inspection of Jonestown. Go and take us with you, and maybe we can make the American ambassador see the light, they said. At least we might get to see our relatives down there, they pleaded.

Ryan was skeptical about all the tales of horror but, as Holsinger said, "Leo knew there was always another side to every story, and his way of finding the truth was to go and look for himself."

In his typically blunt way, Ryan also told the concerned relatives and State Department officials that if there were people being held against their wills at Jonestown, he'd bring them out himself.

In the autumn Holsinger began to plan the trip, but with meticulous care to guarantee that it would be an official visit by a member of the House International Relations Committee—and not the act of one free-wheeling congressman.

Ryan spoke with Committee Chairman Clement Zablocki, a Wisconsin Democrat, who gave the fact-finding trip to Guyana official status and agreed to pay for it out of committee funds.

Ryan also invited other members of the committee to go along, but only one, Representative Edward Derwinski, an Illinois Republican, accepted the invitation. At the last minute, with Ryan waiting at the airport, Derwinski changed his mind.

"Everything was done thoroughly and strictly by the book," said Holsinger. "We wired the U.S. ambassador down there and asked him to make the proper arrangements for an official visit. We even wired Jim Jones on November 1 and told him Leo was coming. It was a conciliatory, mild, nonthreatening telegram."

Word of the Guyana trip was leaked to the press by Holsinger's son, Will Holsinger, an atorney employed by Ryan to do legal research on the Peoples Temple and to explore the possibility that it was violating various United States laws dealing with social security checks and tax-exempt church groups.

The young Holsinger first mentioned the upcoming trip to Gordon Lindsay, a British freelance journalist, who had written several articles about Peoples Temple and was keeping in close contact with Ryan's staff.

Lindsay couldn't go on the trip, but he informed the National Broadcasting Company because the network was preparing a documentary on cults. NBC called Ryan's office and said the network wanted to send a news crew with the congressman. Ryan said OK.

A day or two later, *San Francisco Examiner* reporter Tim Reiterman called Ryan's office. He had learned of the trip from former Peoples Temple members, and he wanted to go, too.

At that point, said Holsinger, he called David Perlman, the *San Francisco Chronicle*'s city editor, and casually mentioned that Ryan was going to Guyana after the election.

Perlman immediately asked if Guyana meant Jonestown and when Holsinger said yes, the *Chronicle* news executive said he wanted to send a reporter along.

"Joe warned us that there was no guarantee that Ryan or anyone else would get any farther than Georgetown," Perlman recalled. "I talked it over with Bill German, our managing editor, and Dick Thieriot, our publisher. We all agreed to send someone."

Perlman decided against sending Marshall Kilduff, the reporter who had written so much about Peoples Temple activities for several years, because Jones and his inner circle considered the persistent young reporter an enemy.

"Frankly, we felt it might not be safe for Marshall down there," said Perlman. "At the very least, he might be harassed. It was also possible that his presence alone might be enough to keep the whole party out of Jonestown."

Instead of Kilduff, Perlman decided to send Ron Javers, a relative newcomer to the city who had never written a word about Peoples Temple in his ten months on the *Chronicle* news staff. He was a former Nieman Fellow at Harvard and primarily a political reporter who had written most of the paper's articles on Proposition 13 and the California tax revolt.

"Ron's an aggressive, energetic, competent reporter," Perlman said later. "He was also essentially unknown to Peoples Temple at that time. That was an important factor in choosing him for the assignment."

Because they had learned of Ryan's trip only a few days before the scheduled departure, the San Francisco reporters didn't have time for the bureaucratic details of securing all the entry permits required for journalists to visit Guyana. They took what steps could be taken at the last minute, but largely went ahead on assurances from Ryan and the Guyanese press office in

Washington that things would be arranged when they arrived in Georgetown.

Holsinger said later that the Guyanese government "did everything they could do to keep the press from going with Leo, while our own State Department stalled and wasn't much interested in helping make the arrangements. They kept telling us that Guyana was a small, sensitive country, and the United States government wanted to avoid any appearance of acting like an insensitive giant.

While the two governments showed so little interest in preparing the way for newsmen to accompany Ryan, the congressman himself assured the reporters, "Trust us. We'll walk you through."

It was a statement typical of Ryan, who could be as imperious as any member of Congress. The big, handsome representative was not someone who suffered fools or stalling bureaucrats—or who ever took no for an answer.

Entry into Guyana on November 14 went smoothly for the entire party—except for the *Chronicle's* Javers. He telephoned Perlman at home late that night from Temehri International Airport in Georgetown and needed help: he was being detained by Guyanese officials, but didn't know why.

First, the officials told Javers his papers weren't in order. Then they said they were holding him at the airport for violating Guyanese currency regulations.

In fact, before leaving San Francisco, Javers had bought 30 Guyanese dollars for $75 in American money.

"It turned out that Guyanese regulations limit travelers to bringing in only $15 Guyanese," Perlman explained later. "After we heard about Ron's problem at the airport, we began a frantic exchange of phone calls with Ryan's office and with the Guyanese embassy in Washington in an effort to straighten things out and get Javers into the country."

At 2:00 a.m., Washington time, Perlman finally reached the home of Representative Philip Burton, a powerful member of Congress and the congressman for most of San Francisco proper.

The blustery Burton, who has been known to tear the hide off a bureaucrat at the slightest provocation, began to make phone calls on Javers's behalf.

A few hours later, a member of the State Department's congressional relations staff called Perlman to assure him that the U.S. embassy in Guyana had been alerted, and that embassy aides were on their way to rescue Javers.

Javers was free from detention, thanks to congressional intervention, and it appeared to the reporters that Ryan was the key to their safe progress. What they didn't know was that Ryan looked upon them in the same way.

"Leo thought the press was his best protection and the press thought he was their protection," Holsinger recalled sadly. "It turned out they were both wrong."

Much later, the grieved congressional aide also recalled a conversation that Ryan had held a few days before the Guyana trip with the members of the NBC film crew that had accompanied him.

"When Leo told them about his experience in Folsom Prison, Bob Brown, the cameraman, asked him what was the most important thing he had learned from the prison visit.

"Leo told them, 'I learned not to be afraid anymore. I found out that you can't give in to fear and get anything done.' "

That was the resolve of Leo J. Ryan. —to investigate realities, to uncover injustices, and not to be afraid. But this time, Ryan, his staff, and the newsmen were about to face the irrational and the unpredictable.

Few eyewitness reports of those brutal hours at Jonestown and Port Kaituma are as vivid as what appears on the following pages. The transcripts are from a tape recording dictated by reporter Ron Javers from a hospital bed at Andrews Air Force Base a day after a Peoples Temple bullet was removed from his shoulder.

11

EYEWITNESS REPORT: GUYANA NOVEMBER 15, 16

In retrospect, being detained for twelve hours by Guyana immigration authorities does not seem like much of an ordeal. Compared to what was to happen later in the week, it was nothing.

But all I knew at the time was that I was

being held by immigration authorities in the middle of the night in a country whose government was not friendly to the United States.

Congressman Ryan, who had said he would help us get into the country safely, had already been whisked away to the United States embassy in Georgetown, thirty miles to the north.

Our Pan American flight, which left New York on the afternoon of Tuesday, November 14, arrived at Temehri International Airport five minutes past midnight on Wednesday morning.

We filed into the low, wooden terminal and waited to pass through immigration and customs. The lines were long and slow, and it was very, very warm. The atmosphere was steamy from the heavy rain that was soaking the field.

The NBC Television crew, which had been working on the story for some time, had their official press permits before they left the United States. They were cleared through the line with a minimum of trouble.

So were Tim Reiterman and Greg Robinson of the *San Francisco Examiner*, who had no permits and whose status seemed exactly like mine. Charles Krause, the *Washington Post* Latin American correspondent, had received his assignment to get to Georgetown only the day before. He, too, got in easily.

When I reached the head of the line, my passport was taken away, and so was the money I had purchased from Deak & Co. in San Francisco to cover any expenses I might have before I could get to a bank—330 Guyana dollars, or about $75 in U.S. currency.

The corporal in charge stamped my passport

NOT PERMITTED TO LAND. He would give no explanation.

Khaki-clad uniformed guards took me into a room fifteen feet by fifteen feet and told me to wait.

Airline officials attempted to help. Pan Am offered to take responsibility for my custody overnight, first at a hotel in Georgetown and then, after officials rejected that proposal, in a courtesy room that Pan Am maintains at the airport.

By then everybody in the party had left except for Bob Flick of NBC. Flick said he intended to remain at my side as long as necessary.

We sat on a tattered green plastic sofa and talked.

One of the guards assigned to watch over me soon fell alseep. I envied him, but there was no sleep for me. The adrenaline was flowing, and I never felt less sleepy in my life.

At 3:20 a.m. the immigration corporal asked Flick if the producer would—"as a special favor to the immigration authorities"—drive one of the officers to Georgetown in Flick's rental car.

Flick tossed the corporal the keys to the car and said he was staying.

At 3:30 a.m. a lone woman began sweeping up the day's litter. At 4:30 a.m. the corporal, eager to go home, returned for a few moments. He had changed out of his uniform and donned an aloha shirt, a pair of slacks, and a baseball cap.

By now the second guard in charge of my custody had fallen asleep, but there seemed to be no point in trying to escape.

There was no place to go.

At 5:30 a.m. a workman arrived to run up the red, yellow, and green flag of the Republic of Guyana.

Shortly before 6:30 we were getting some daylight. We could see the Pan Am 707 that had brought us here and an old, propeller-driven Cubana airliner, the only other airliner on the field. Guyana, with its socialist government, maintains close ties with Cuba.

We were still waiting at 8:20 a.m., when my old guards left and a new force led by a uniformed man with epaulets took over. It took until 10:55 a.m. before one of the guards on the day shift fell asleep.

By then I had been given permission to go to the airport coffee shop. I was looking forward to eating a good breakfast, but the coffee shop turned out to be precisely what the name indicates; it sold coffee and nothing else.

At 11:20 a.m. I was summoned to the Pan Am desk to take a call from Ryan, who assured me, "I've done everything I can, and I'm going to keep pushing."

While Ryan was pressing the case at Georgetown, Congressman Phillip Burton of San Francisco had learned of my plight. He was in Washington, pounding the State Department for action.

At noon I was summoned into the immigration director's office, and for the first time I saw a Guyanese official smiling. The director said he was sorry about any difficulties I had encountered. But now he had received instructions to let me enter. I could stay in the country for five days.

He stamped my passport, and Flick and I rode off in a taxi on the two-lane curving highway that parallels the Demerara river up the coast to Georgetown.

When we arrived, we discovered things had not gone too well for our colleagues either. They found, when they reached the Pegasus Hotel, that reservations had been mysteriously canceled, causing many of them to spend as sleepless a night as Bob Flick's and mine.

Immigration officials arrived at the hotel long before daybreak—apparently that was why they had taken Flick's rental car—to tell Tim Reiterman and Greg Robinson that entry permits had been stamped in their passports by mistake.

They were instructed to get out of Guyana on the 1:00 p.m. flight to New York—an order that was canceled at the same time I got permission to stay.

Our reservations at the Pegasus, the best hotel in town, were suddenly reconfirmed. I could hardly wait for the midday shutdown of the hotel's running water to end so I could freshen up.

But being in Georgetown was only the first step. And there were times when it seemed that might be as far as we would get.

Negotiations were getting nowhere.

The fourteen relatives of Temple members who had accompanied Ryan on the flight from New York were becoming impatient and upset.

A group of them went Wednesday afternoon to the Peoples Temple's outpost in Georgetown, a large wood and stucco building where about twenty members of the organization lived.

They were met at the gate by three women they knew—women from the San Francisco Bay Area who had followed Jim Jones to Guyana.

"None of you are welcome," a member told the visitors, barring the gate. "Go see the American ambassador."

That was what Ryan was doing. As the ambassador's houseguest, he began the day with a briefing on Jonestown, complete with color slides.

What he saw was impressive, Ryan acknowledged, but it was no substitute for getting there. He wasn't at all satisfied with the assurances he was being offered at the embassy.

"I came to investigate the conditions of people who I have been told are working from dawn to nightfall with terrible mental and physical punishments if they don't work hard enough," the congressman told the press that evening.

"The Peoples Temple seeks to delay us and to try to wait us out."

Ryan had spent part of the day in what was to be a round of long-distance telephone negotiations with Charles Garry of San Francisco and Mark Lane, of assassination-conspiracy fame, two lawyers competing for the right to represent Jim Jones and the Temple.

The Georgetown Temple issued a brief statement condemning Ryan's planned visit as "a contrived media event."

The negotiations continued Thursday, with Ryan trying to maintain an open posture toward Jones.

"Jim Jones might have something going there,"

Ryan said. "The pictures of the place indicate he may have worked wonders, cutting through the jungle and establishing that community. But I want to know if Pat and Judy are out there clearing that land by hand."

He was referring to two granddaughters of his longtime friend, Associated Press photographer Sam Houston of San Francisco.

"My assumptions about the place may be unfair," the congressman continued, "or they may be the stark truth."

I hired a car and driver Thursday morning and took a twenty-minute trip from the center of Georgetown to the local Peoples Temple in the Lamaha Gardens section. The relatives had been turned away, but perhaps I could get in.

We crossed dirt roads where men and women herded fat cows in the streets. We saw orderly rows of dark-skinned schoolchildren in their neat maroon and gold uniforms.

We pulled up to the building's low, open gate, and I called but, "Hello."

Two teenagers took me inside the house to a clean, orderly bedroom, where several other youths, Americans like my guides, sat chatting on bunks.

On a side porch, I was introduced to Sharon Amos, a small, pleasant woman of early middle age. At first she didn't want to talk. After all, I had come to her house uninvited, and I was one of the first reporters ever to go there.

"How can we print your side of the Peoples Temple story if we cannot see you and talk?"

Things brightened up a bit then, and I met Jim Jones's son Stephan, dressed in camouflage fatigues rolled up to his knees. While Sharon Amos and I talked, Jones worked out with a set of barbells.

John Cobb and three other teenage youths, dressed in shorts and athletic shirts, were on their way to practice basketball. John's brother, Jim, was one of the relatives who had flown to Georgetown with Ryan.

I met Debbie Touchette, a smiling young black woman. Her sister, Micki, had flown down to find out what had happened to her mother, father, grandmother, grandfather, two brothers, an uncle, and Debbie—eight people in all.

We were to learn more about many of these people later, but in the meantime I listened to Sharon Amos. She told me the press was biased against Jones, a man she said had done nothing but good all his life.

"It's not just those relatives," she said, referring to the people who had been turned away, "but it's a conspiracy to destroy the Peoples Temple."

As we talked, her nine-year-old son, Martin, played at his mother's feet.

I left after about forty-five minutes and said I hoped to be able to see Jonestown and learn the facts firsthand.

By Thursday night, Ryan was weary of the frustration of dealing on the phone with Mark Lane. The negotiations seemed to be going nowhere.

And we were getting impatient. We called on Ryan to complain about the lack of cooperation on the part of both U.S. embassy and Guyanese officials.

Don Harris of NBC, who had covered the fall of Saigon from the roof of the American embassy, said, "I don't know about you fellows, but I came here to see Jonestown and, one way or another, I am going."

Bob Flick, in charge of logistics for the NBC team, had arranged to charter planes in Guyana and nearby countries, and Reiterman and I agreed to share in the charter.

Ryan told us to bear with him. He thought a break was coming.

But it had been a discouraging day.

The frustrated relatives had been demanding a meeting with U.S. Ambassador John R. Burke, and thanks to Ryan's intervention they finally were admitted to the modest white stucco embassy, tucked in next to a row of decaying storefronts on Main Street.

The press was barred, so we amused ourselves by doing a little shopping and seeing whether, as an old Pan Am tour book put it, Georgetown was "the garden city of South America."

Back in front of the embassy, Bob Brown, the NBC cameraman, captivated a small, ragged bunch of kids by letting them look through his TV camera at the passing traffic.

The relatives emerged from the embassy after an hour and a half.

Howard Oliver, a San Francisco watchmaker whose two teenage sons had been in Jonestown for over a year, described the sessions as "more of the same old embassy runaround."

His wife, Beverly, forty-seven, was more blunt: "Bullshit!"

As Burke stepped into a brown car and prepared to drive away, he told reporters he thought of the talks as "useful"—a word that I concluded was a meaningless, though doubtless useful, piece of diplomatic double-talk.

Ryan was getting as impatient as we were. Thursday night he went out to the Georgetown Peoples Temple. He asked Charles Krause of the *Washington Post* to drive out with him and wait in the car as a witness.

"I walked in there," the congressman told us later, "and I simply said, 'Hi, I'm Leo Ryan, the bad guy. Does anyone want to talk?'

There were about a dozen people present, mostly young men, seated around a table. Other people closed their doors as he approached. Sharon Amos was there and Jim McElvane, a large black man who was clearly in charge.

It was astonishing, Ryan said. Only he, Sharon Amos, and McElvane said anything. The twelve young men didn't talk at all—not to him or to each other.

"I told them, 'I don't want the warden's two-dollar tour—I want to talk to the people there,'" Ryan continued.

"I said, 'If I'm satisfied that the testimony of relatives about bad conditions is untrue, then there is no basis to the charges. On the other hand, if you refuse entry to me, then this is a prison. There are social security laws involved here, finance and tax laws, as well as passport regulations, and I intend to pursue that through every area of the U.S. government.'"

Ryan was getting tougher as time passed.

"I don't want intermediaries," he said. "The Geneva convention rules on prisoners require that face-to-face contact be made. Anybody who denies access to the press or to legitimate government inquiry denies basic constitutional rights."

Then the congressman reflected on something we had overlooked.

"You know," he told us, "I have not heard anybody from the Temple once mention God. There are no elements of religious life present in that house. If this is not a religious institution, why are they tax-exempt? There is a posturing of religious life, but I am not sure it exists."

The officials at Peoples Temple had told Ryan that Jim Jones was too ill to see him, even if he flew in alone. They said only Mark Lane could make the arrangements.

So the lawyers were in command after all.

It was now Friday morning. Mark Lane and Charles Garry had arrived from the United States. And we were all gathered in the lobby of the Pegasus Hotel.

Ryan, the press, and the relatives had chipped in to charter a plane, and we were eager to start the 150-mile flight to the airstrip at Port Kaituma, six miles east of Jonestown.

"Just give us two hours to talk to Jonestown to see if they want you to come in," Lane kept shouting.

"You're stalling, Mark, you're stalling," Ryan's aide, Jackie Speier, replied. "Let's get this show on the road."

Meanwhile Garry told me, "Mark and I affirmatively want you there. We want the press there."

At that moment, I am sure, Garry was convinced that once we got to Jonestown, we would share with him the believe that the place was, in fact, "a paradise."

We rode out to the airport.

Eyewitness Report
November 17, 18

Finally we were on our way to Jonestown. We were leaving the unsettling inactivity of Georgetown, a languid capital of 180,000 that looked and seemed like the setting of a Graham Greene novel of tropical intrigue, a place where nothing happens most of the time but where anything can happen sometimes.

Now the story would have a deeper, darker dimension. We were flying over dense, green jungle into a setting that bore an awesome resemblance to that of Eugene O'Neill's chilling drama with the oddly prophetic title *The Emperor Jones.*

"Ain't I de Emperor?" O'Neill's Jones asks in the 1920 work. "De laws don't go for him."

The accents are different. O'Neill's Jones came from Harlem to take over command of a tropical colony. San Francisco's Jones was a product of Middle America, but he, too, kept his followers in thrall.

I recalled that the Emperor Jones dies in a rain of silver bullets.

No one could predict then what would happen to Jim Jones, but we had all heard the stories of the mass suicide drills. It seemed safe to guess that however he died, it wouldn't be of old age.

It was a flight of a little over an hour, and

there were eighteen of us in the chartered Twin Otter from Guyana Airways.

Ryan was the leader, the man whose presence made the trip possible. Then there were the two lawyers, Lane and Garry, who had succeeded in persuading Jones that he couldn't bar the Jonestown gates to a visiting congressman on an official mission. Lane and Garry served another function. We thought of them as our assurances of safe-conduct.

And then there were the rest of us, the small party of press, two aides of Ryan's staff, American embassy and Guyana government officials, and four members of the Concerned Relatives party. By now we had taken to capitalizing the words, at least mentally, as though the Concerned Relatives were a formal, established organization.

We were especially taken by Anthony Katsaris, a sad-eyed, mustachioed man from Ukiah who looked younger than his twenty-three years. Katsaris had flown to Georgetown with his father in the hope that the two of them could persuade Anthony's twenty-five-year-old sister, Maria, to return home.

James Cobb, twenty-eight, seemed steady and self-assured. A San Francisco dental student, he had been a member of the Peoples Temple from 1967 to 1973. In 1972 he had been sent by the organization to take a course at the San Francisco Police Academy covering powers of arrest and the carrying and use of firearms. He hoped to find his mother, three sisters, and two brothers in Jonestown.

Beverly Oliver of San Francisco had flown to Georgetown with her husband, Howard, hoping to bring back two sons, Bruce, nineteen, and Billy, eighteen.

Carol Boyd, daughter of Associated Press photographer Sam Houston, was the fourth. She had flown to Georgetown with her mother, Nadyne Houston, to seek out her brother's children, Patricia, fifteen, and Judy, fourteen.

There was no space for anyone else. Ten members of the Concerned Relatives had to stay behind in Georgetown and wait. The group had held a painful meeting at the Pegasus Hotel and concluded it was more important for the press to send out firsthand reports than it was for them to have long-delayed family reunions.

They had selected the four members of the group who represented them.

The plane continued on. At some points the trees were so thick we couldn't see the ground, and like everyone who flies over the jungle, I wondered for a moment or so how we could survive a forced landing. Elsewhere there were large stretches of flat, deep, red mud.

There were no roads. It was startling to realize how isolated people could be only 150 miles from the capital. There was no way to get to Jonestown except by air or by a long boat trip along the Atlantic coast and up the Kaituma River. I felt a little trapped.

We were nearing our destination. The flying weather was good, and when we emerged from clouds, we could see rainbows shining below us. Perhaps, I thought without much conviction, it was a hopeful sign.

But then reality intruded. The plane landed on the airstrip at Port Kaituma. When the steward threw down the loading steps, we found a single-shot, 30-gauge shotgun pointing right into our faces.

There were two men. The man with the gun identified himself as Corporal Rudder of the Guyanese police. He said we were refused permission to land.

Even Lane and Garry were taken aback by this. They thought they had worked out an arrangement with Jones by radio.

"Who gave you these instructions?" we asked.

"The people at Peoples Temple gave me these instructions several days ago," the corporal said. "I think if you go up there, there will be trouble. I think if you go there, people will be shot."

Corporal Rudder put his gun aside, and we all stepped out of the plane to continue negotiations. Rudder was a small man of exceptional ugliness, but we discovered he could be fairly charming when he wasn't pointing a gun at us.

A tractorload of people had come out to the airstrip from Jonestown to meet the plane. It was decided that Lane and Garry could ride back with them to negotiate.

We waited a half hour beside the red mud and cinder runway in the ninety-degree heat. Someone sold us a couple of cases of ice-cold beer.

Then a big, ten-wheeled, yellow dump truck lumbered up to us, and we were told to climb aboard for the ride through foot-thick mud to Jonestown.

It was raining when we sloshed past the gate

and a small hut with several people inside. By the time we reached the settlement in the center of the colony, night had already fallen.

We were escorted to the pavilion, a large central gathering hall with a tin roof and open sides. We walked past one of the poles holding up the roof and were seated at a long table on the packed earth floor.

Jim Jones was sitting at the head of the table, dressed in a red shirt and khaki pants. He had black hair and long sideburns, and even though it was night, he was wearing sunglasses. He always wore them, we learned.

Immediately he looked to me like a man who was powdered and perfumed. He was sweating a bit on his upper lip and forehead and complaining about his illness. He said he had a temperature of 103 degrees.

I told myself I was looking at a man in decay.

I wasn't prepared to reach a conclusion yet about precisely what was wrong, but I was severely troubled.

They offered us coffee, and later we were given a dinner of barbecused pork, collard greens, potato salad, and coffee. As we were eating, it crossed my mind how easy it would be for Jim Jones to poison us all here and now. But, of course, we kept eating.

Later, as the night wore on, an excellent rock band performed for us. The show was lively and entertaining, and the emotional content was thick and heavy—and unreal. We watched, but we were isolated from the rest of the audience.

It seemed forced and unnatural for elderly

people, many of them middle-class whites, to be stamping their feet, yelling, and clapping their hands to music that only a younger generation could understand. I thought they might be under orders to be enthusiastic.

Then several young Jonestown men and women and a comedienne, an old woman they called Jonestown's Moms Mabley, sang for us. All of them, surprisingly, were first-rate.

Ryan was called on to say a few words.

"I'm very glad to be here," the congressman said, the spotlight shining on him as he addressed the crowd. "Despite the charges I have heard about Jonestown, I am sure there are some people here this evening who believe this is the best thing that ever happened to them in their whole lives."

Pandemonium broke out. Three solid minutes of standing ovation, shouting, and cheering.

"I feel terrible that you all can't register to vote in San Mateo County," Ryan added when the shouting died down.

But after that wan joke, he turned stern.

"I want to pull no punches," Ryan said unsmilingly. "This is a congressional inquiry."

I tried to break away from the group and find someone to talk to, but all I could find were people bobbing and nodding and assuring me that everybody was having a wonderful time.

At eleven o'clock the show ended and the audience vanished into the clapboard houses surrounding the pavilion.

But the facade finally cracked a little. A woman from Jonestown managed to edge up to

Don Harris of NBC and slip him a note with this dark message: "Please help us get out of Jonestown."

There were four signatures, written with a black Magic Marker.

Harris slipped the note into the top of his boot.

Now the pavilion was deserted except for Jones, some of his top lieutenants, and our small party.

We were told we would have to get out. Ryan and the two lawyers could spend the night at Jonestown, but we were informed there was no room for us in the entire settlement.

We argued. We wanted to lay out our sleeping bags in the empty pavilion or on the ground outside it. Anywhere. But this was impossible, we were told. The Peoples Temple had reserved space for us at the home of a man named Mike who ran a discotheque in Port Kaituma. We would be picked up at 8:30 the following morning to continue our visit.

There was nothing we could do. We climbed into the truck and arrived at Mike's house at midnight. The women in the group were offered the bedroom, and the men were told they could sleep in the living room and on the kitchen floor.

The press retired to the disco, a corrugated-tin-roof affair with a small, rickety record player and five or six reggae records. The walls were painted with iridescent paint and slogans like "Hey-O, Baby," "Soul Time," and "Play That Music."

We drank some beer out on the patio and talked. We were deeply discouraged.

At four o'clock the young policeman who had accompanied Corporal Rudder came out and indicated to Tim Reiterman of the *San Francisco Examiner* and me that he had something important to say in private.

We followed him out a long, muddy road along a set of rusty railroad tracks laid when there was a big manganese mine in operation at Matthews Ridge, thirty miles to the south. He led us to a small shack by the river. It was pitch-dark, and we had to feel our way in with our hands.

Then a second man struck a match and a candle in a beer can. Together they told us about a man named Leon.

Several Guyanese had found Leon in the summer of 1977 after he had escaped from Jonestown, they said. He had been kept in "the hold," a large pit a quarter of a mile behind the kitchen area at Jonestown.

The policeman said he had seen the hold himself and, inside it, the small black box where prisoners who had violated the code of Jim Jones were condemned to spend time for punishment. There was no light. No air. No sound, even.

The policeman wouldn't go back. Even though it was Guyanese territory and he was a Guyanese official, the foreigners in their midst kept too tight a guard. But he told us how to find the place.

Thanks to friendly Guyanese who passed him

along from one helper to another, Leon had managed to make good his escape. He returned to San Francisco and talked to several reporters, none of whom knew whether or not to believe him. His story was too fantastic, and it was impossible to check.

Now here we were, hearing the same account, this time from a Guyanese policeman.

I had heard similar, less graphic stories from other young Guyanese, who took me aside and told me privately that they had seen people from Jonestown with broken arms and broken hands. They had also heard stories of beatings.

"People do try to get out," one man told us. Sometimes the escape attempts occurred twice a year, sometimes twice a month.

"They try to hide this," the man went on, "but we see it. People around here are not so low as they think."

We returned to the disco and dozed for a few hours.

We were ready at 8:30, but the promised truck did not appear. At nine o'clock Don Harris gave us cups of instant coffee he made from powder he carried in a container of survival gear.

Still nothing at 9:30

Reiterman and I decided to tell Harris what we had learned from the young policeman.

Harris in turn showed us the plea for help that he had received. He was going to pass it on to Ryan.

We were all highly competitive by nature,

but we had decided by this time that we were competing with Jones, not with each other.

Ten o'clock came. Nothing.

But at 10:30 the big yellow truck returned to carry us back the six miles to Jonestown.

We were offered breakfast on our arrival. We said no thanks, we wanted to go to work and look around.

Our tour was tightly guided. Marceline Jones, the minister's wife and a former nurse, took us to the children's nursery. It was a bright little cabin done up with murals and hand-drawn decorations.

Half a dozen youngsters played on a side patio shaded from the sun. Several women looked on.

We were then shown to a classroom where fifteen or twenty kids sat and practiced reading. This seemed odd. It was a Saturday, and we had been told Jonestown maintained a normal school schedule—Monday to Friday.

Whenever we tried to break away from the things we thought had been organized especially for our visit, someone would pop up and offer to guide us.

"Hi," the person would say in the cheeriest of voices, "can I help you?"

Still, we were managing to get some idea of what the place looked like. There were large field kitchens with poles holding up corrugated metal roofs.

The place was crisscrossed with paths of some light asphalt material laid in the mud. They had four-foot-high railings along the sides.

The central pavilion was surrounded by white and gray clapboard buildings.

The strained friendliness stopped when some of us left our guides and approached a building called Jane Pittman Gardens. The shutters of the twenty-by-forty-foot barracks were drawn, and the door was barred.

We knocked lightly on the door, and an old woman's face peeked through the crack.

"Please don't come in here," she said. "We don't want to see anybody."

She shut the door.

We turned to our guides, who said they wanted to respect the old woman's right to privacy. They told us many of the women inside had been raped or robbed back in the United States and were terrified of strangers.

We appealed to Garry and Lane. They had assured us we could see what Jonestown was like, and now the door was barred. The lawyers intervened, and a moment later, when we were allowed into the barracks, we could see why no one in command wanted to show off Jane Pittman Gardens.

There were sixty bunks or more, double- and triple-tiered. Thirty old women were sitting on them, and we could see others scurrying out the back door. Almost all were black.

I talked to about ten of the old women. All seemed horribly frightened. They assured me, in the saddest, most timorous tones imaginable, that they were very, very happy—that they were living in paradise.

The picture was cracking.

One woman, Edith Parks, walked up to Don

Harris and said in a firm, clear voice, "I want to go with you. I want to leave Jonestown."

"You can come with us," Harris replied. "You'll be safe."

He took her to Congressman Ryan, who told her to sit on a bench until we were ready to leave.

Jones walked over and asked if he could talk to her.

"Of course," Ryan replied.

The atmosphere changed. Jones became agitated. He talked intensely into her ear. We couldn't hear the words, but obviously he was urgently trying to make her change her mind.

The old woman would have none of it. She stared ahead, her hands squeezed together in her lap, and she didn't reply.

Jones seemed to be growing desperate. Sweat broke out on his forehead. We watched the scene in fascination.

At this point we noticed that several more people were getting up courage to say they wanted to go.

The list grew.

About an hour before it was time for us to leave Jonestown, nine people had said they wanted to go.

Then twelve.

Finally about twenty were ready to defy Jones.

Dick Dwyer, the deputy chief of mission from the U.S. embassy in Georgetown, was getting worried. He knew we had only an eighteen-seat plane coming for sure and possibly a four-seat plane as well.

What would happen to those who had to be left behind?

It was decided we would have to make a couple of trips. Members of the press, the Concerned Relatives, and some Jonestown refugees were instructed to climb aboard the dump truck when it took its first run to Port Kaituma.

Congressman Ryan would leave on the second trip.

Eyewitness Report:
Interview with Jim Jones, November 18

"I reject violence," Jim Jones told us. "I reject corporal and physical punishment."

He spoke in a low, slow drawl, and he was trying hard to convince us, as he had convinced so many other people.

He appeared both frightened and fascinated by the press during the hours we were permitted to spend in Jonestown.

At first he seemed to be trying to keep us talking to him so that we wouldn't have time to get information from anyone else.

But then we seemed to pose a personal challenge. He wanted to sweep away our skepticism.

We had heard too many stories about beatings to accept Jones's assurances without further questioning. We asked about one young girl who had been pounded seventy-five times with a large board.

Photographs showing Linda Mertle's bloody and bruised backside had been smuggled out of Jonestown, and we had seen them before we arrived.

"We don't use physical punishment anymore," Jones replied. "We stopped it a few months ago—maybe a year."

But what about the photographs?

"The girl got the seventy-five spankings because her mother, Mrs. Mertle, began it herself.

The girl was a kleptomaniac. Her mother demanded that punishment.

"I said to her mother, 'You spank me first.' I often took spankings."

Nowadays, Jones tried to convince us, punishment consisted of a withdrawal of privileges or exclusion from work.

I asked about the so-called catharsis sessions, where members of the colony would hurl abuse, both physical and psychological, on other members for hours at a time.

"We had it," Jones answered, "but not anymore."

We talked about guns.

"There are no guns at all, to my knowledge," Jones began.

John Brown, one of Jones's so-called adopted children, joined in to say that even when the men went hunting, they never used guns—only, he insisted, bows and arrows.

We found repeatedly that if one answer didn't seem to convince us, Jones was ready to try another.

There were, he acknowledged, some weapons—"but only rifles and hunting guns."

And finally, as our first hour-long interview drew to a close, "Guns, yes. But how many, I don't know."

There was, as we suspected, an arsenal.

The man was clearly the absolute ruler of his 27,000-acre domain. His subjects called him Father, and he called himself the Father.

We asked why it was that people were willing to turn over total control of their lives to him.

"I am a socialist who believes in absolute democracy," Jones responded.

"What the hell kind of power do I have out here? They say I want power. What kind of power is it out here, walking along the streets with my seniors?"

He was getting vehement by now.

"I hate power. I don't want money. The only thing I want now is to have never been born. I feel more so every day. I'm not worried about my image anymore. I want to have never been born."

There was a pause, and the man who said he didn't care about his image told us he had let the press enter Jonestown only because he had been coerced by his lawyers, Mark Lane and Charles Garry.

"I have doubts you can print the truth," Jones said. "If you printed the truth, you'd be in trouble. The press has open season on anybody who has any kind of adversary life-style."

Suddenly Jones ordered John Victor Stoen, Grace Stoen's son, to be brought over to us so the child could be displayed before the TV camera. Both Jones and Tim Stoen claimed to be the father of the handsome six-year-old boy.

"Show 'em your teeth," Jones told the boy. "Show 'em your profile. See, he looks exactly like me."

The bewildered, dark-haired child did as he was told, baring his teeth and turning his head.

"It's not right to play with children's lives," Jones went on. "Yes, I believe that."

Tim Stoen and his estranged wife, Grace, had both flown to Georgetown with the other

Concerned Relatives. Both were waiting there now.

Jones said Grace had been one of his mistresses for four or five years.

"Grace showed no interest in that child until it got in the papers," Jones told me. "Grace is a tear-jerker, a great actress. The day she left San Francisco, she asked to marry me. I said, 'I can't. I'm married twenty-seven years myself to Marceline.'

"Grace is a seductive female, a terrible female. I feel a great deal of guilt about this relationship."

We said we had heard that sex was his special privilege at Jonestown—that everyone else was required to maintain strict celibacy.

"No sex?" he answered. "Bullshit. Bullshit. Bullshit. Thirty babies have been born since the summer of 1977 in Jonestown. How could we have babies if we didn't have sex?"

There were moments when the talk seemed rational. We discussed the development of the 27,000-acre commune. So far, he said, most of it was still jungle, but Jonestown's settlers had cleared perhaps as much as 10,000 acres.

Their food still came in mostly from the United States, Jones said, partly because early, heavy rains were going to leave the colony with light crops of plantains, oranges, and green vegetables.

Though meat had been served up to the visitors, we had been able to learn that the diet for the residents was often just rice and gravy, three times a day.

"This is a model community," Jones went on.

"People come in here all the time. There is rarely a day when we don't have a visitor."

But abruptly the brave talk took a different turn.

"I feel like a man without a country. Sure, I want to come back to the United States. As soon as I get these lawsuits out of the way, I will."

We waited. There was no need to ask questions just now, and Jones continued.

"I am sick. In many ways I feel like I am dying. I've got to get to a hospital, but I have too many responsibilities here. I had pneumonia until five days ago. I have a temperature of 103. My lungs, my kidneys, cancer—who knows?"

The interviews took another turn shortly before our departure on the second day.

"Obviously there is a conspiracy," Jones declared. "Somebody shot at me."

I asked who was in the conspiracy.

"Who conspired to kill Martin Luther King, John F. Kennedy, and Malcolm X?" he demanded.

"Every agency in the U.S. government has given me a hard time. I have tried to build a community that is an alternative to the culture of the United States. I took street addicts and dope pushers and I brought them out here, and I have been successful. Whoever is conspiring to destroy the Peoples Temple is foolish. It's foolish to destroy voluntary socialist society."

His vehemence was increasing.

"Why would anybody be afraid of me? People are killing me with that kid of rubbish!"

He asked all the news people for assurance that we would tell about the Jonestown residents who were happy as well as about those who were leaving.

We replied that NBC cameras and the newspaper reporters had already conducted interviews with people who said they wanted to remain.

"I've given my life for my people," Jones said. "I live for the people and I try to serve them!"

He sounded hysterical.

As we and the dissidents gathered in the pavilion before making our way to the dump truck for our trip to the airstrip, Jones complained, "Every time people chose to leave in the past, they chose to lie. People lied to me when they said they didn't want to leave—and then they left.

"Let's hope it doesn't happen again."

It was going to be a wet departure. The rain was smashing against the pavilion roof.

Jones realized for the first time, it seemed, how many there were who wanted to get away.

"Excuse me," he told the reporters. "I want to hug them all before they leave."

Eyewitness Report: November 18, 19

To our great relief, we were finally aboard the truck for the ride from Jonestown to the airstrip.

Suddenly we heard a commotion in the pavilion where we had left Leo Ryan and Lane and Garry.

A cheer rang through the crowd.

The newsmen scrambled down onto the muddy roadway to see what was happening. The frightened dissidents, hoping to ride to freedom with us, stayed aboard.

We dashed toward the assembly area. A bunch of tough-looking young security guards blocked the way. They ordered us back on the truck.

Then we saw Ryan, blood all over the front of his shirt, being led briskly back to the truck. Lane was holding him by the arm.

Ryan's face was as white as his hair.

Lane helped Ryan climb aboard and told us he and Garry would stay behind with another batch of dissidents who hoped to get away. He said they would try to calm the enraged members of the Peoples Temple.

"Get out—fast!" Lane shouted.

But our driver was from the Peoples Temple too, and he was in no hurry. The yellow, ten-wheeled dump truck moved slowly from the scene.

We could see Lane waving at us as we reached a bend.

We gathered around Ryan in the back of the open truck.

A young man had run out of the crowd, he said, and tried to stab him.

The knife was at Ryan's throat when Lane and Garry grabbed the attacker by the arm and seized the weapon.

Ryan wasn't cut. The blood came from his attacker—later identified as Donald Sly—who was slashed while he was being disarmed.

Ryan wasn't our only last-minute passenger. Larry Layton, a wild, nervous-looking man climbed aboard and said he wanted to escape from Jonestown.

The other fugitives were terrified.

"He is one of his lieutenants. He is one of the higher-ups," they said. "He'll kill us all, he'll kill us all."

We dismissed their pleas. We had said anyone who wanted to go would leave with us, and he had as much right to get away as they did.

Now at 4:20 p.m. on Saturday, November 18, we could see the two planes waiting for us, the Otter we had chartered the day before and the smaller, single-engine Cessna, which could carry away some of the people hoping to escape.

We knew we had to get out as fast as we could.

But we weren't fast enough.

From the far end of the field and to our left came the Peoples Temple dump truck we had left, with a red tractor and trailer partially shielded behind it.

Three or four men jumped off.

And then the shooting started.

I was standing between two NBC men, Bob

Brown and Don Harris. We had become close friends in the course of our trip.

I was hit first. I was knocked to the ground by a slug in the left shoulder from a .38-caliber weapon.

I crawled behind the right wheel of the plane.

Don Harris was hit.

Bob Brown, the NBC cameraman, tried to stay on his feet and keep filming even as the gunmen advanced.

He was incredibly tenacious.

One or two gunmen stepped in with big guns. Then I saw one of the attackers stick a shotgun right into Brown's face—inches away, if that.

Bob's brain was splattered all over his blue NBC minicam.

I saw Don Harris shot at close range.

I jumped up and ran across the airstrip as fast as I've ever run in my life. I remember thinking to zigzag so I wouldn't be an easy target in the short grass. But I also remember thinking, No, it will slow you down. Run straight. I dived into the jungle, tearing scratches into my hands and arms, knocking my glasses off my face and my camera from my neck. I was sure the men could follow me.

Panting for breath, I made my way fifty yards into the undergrowth. Then I stopped. I was in swamp up to my waist. It's time to take inventory, I told myself.

Very purposefully, I took my handkerchief out of my pocket and wadded it against my upper left shoulder where I'd been hit. My khaki-colored shirt was already drenched in blood.

Carefully, I tied my shoes, which had come loose in the thick mud. Somehow I collected my wits. Night would fall in about an hour, and I would never get out if I went deeper into the swamp. I decided to travel parallel to the airport runway so that I would have some notion of where I was. I moved through the swamp until I was about three hundred yards from where we were attacked.

I worked my way into the tall grass at the edge of the runway. And carefully, ever so carefully, I peered through the grass at the plane.

The smaller plane, mercifully, had got away.

I made out the white cap worn by Bob Flick of NBC and the red and maroon polo shirt that the *Examiner* reporter Tim Reiterman had been wearing.

I ran out on the runway.

As I got closer, I could see that Reiterman's arm was shattered.

Both men were obviously dazed.

Congressman Ryan was lying in the mud in front of the right wheel of the aircraft.

His face had been shot off.

Don Harris lay alongside the middle of the plane.

Bob Brown's body was at the tail.

Patricia Parks, the daughter of the woman who had defied Jones and insisted on leaving, was lying at the foot of the plane's stairs.

Greg Robinson, the brilliant young *San Francisco Examiner* photographer in our party, was at the left wheel, his body almost jackknifed.

By this time survivors were moving some of the most seriously wounded off the airstrip and into the brush.

We needed cover. We were sure the killers would come back to finish us off.

We tried to stop the bleeding as best we could. I remember stuffing napkins, towels, anything we could get hold of, into those massive, gaping wounds. We poured rum on some of the wounds, and the bandages in our small first-aid kit were quickly exhausted—swallowed up in bile and blood.

Then we settled in the tall grass to wait for darkness to fall. It wouldn't be far off.

Our hope was that we could last out the night until rescuers arrived.

We knew, of course, that the pilot of the small plane must have radioed for help as soon as he got clear. But there were no lights at the Port Kaituma airstrip, and it seemed unlikely that the Guyanese military would risk a night landing.

Still, some local Guyanese brought out oil pots to mark the edges of the runway. They told us it would be just ten or fifteen minutes—an hour at the very most—before help arrived.

It was impossible to estimate how much time was passing, but most of us realized we were going to have to wait much, much longer than that.

Fifty or sixty Guyanese had come out from the bush and the nearby settlement of Port Kaituma. Some approached and offered us aid. Others took watches, tape recorders, and electronic gear from the bodies before we could chase them away.

I saw two Guyanese walking up to Dick Dwyer, the deputy chief of mission at the American embassy in Georgetown. Between them they had Larry Layton, Jones's thirty-two-year-old lieutenant who had climbed into our truck just before Ryan arrived.

Dale Parks, whose wife, Patricia, had been killed in the raid at the airstrip, told what happened.

Layton had managed to force his way onto the small Cessna, he said, and fire four shots with a handgun. He had hit two of the fugitives from Jonestown.

Then Parks had dragged him out of the little plane and managed to grab the gun. Parks had pulled the trigger, but nothing happened. The gun was jammed.

I told the Guyanese guards to get Layton away from the fugitives from the Peoples Temple. They were ready to tear him apart.

Dwyer, who took charge of our battered little party, stuck the pistol in the pocket of his bush jacket.

Then we realized we had not been alone when the shooting took place.

The gunmen had waved away the Guyanese who had come to see us take off. And four Guyanese soldiers, armed with submachine guns, had watched the action from 200 yards away.

They told us they hadn't dared to shoot during the attack because they were afraid they would kill still more people.

They had watched the gunmen drive off in

their tractor and had let them go without firing a round.

The only policeman at the field, carrying the familiar single-shot shotgun that had greeted us the day before, had been disarmed by the killers the moment the attack began.

We approached the Guyanese soldiers now.

Dick Dwyer persuaded them to let us put our most seriously wounded in their tent.

Villagers said the rest of us, including some less seriously wounded like Tim Reiterman and me, could wait in a small cafe called a rum house.

It was dark and stormy.

We took turns, two at a time, staying in the tent to care for the wounded.

Jackie Speier, Ryan's aide, was tremendously brave. She had about half her thigh shot away, and she suffered massive wounds in her arm and chest. Yet somehow she managed to get her tape recorder going and make a tape.

She pulled my ear close to her lips and whispered, "Ron, I know I'm going to make it, but in case I don't, please give this tape to my parents."

"Sure, you're going to make it," I said. "Deliver the tape yourself."

"I know, I know," she replied, "but you take it anyway."

I buttoned it in the top pocket of my shirt and carried it with me through that long, long night.

Anthony Katsaris, who had spent long, earnest hours trying to persuade his sister, Maria, to return, had been hit very badly. We tried giving him water and then Pepsi-Cola. That was all we had except rum and beer. He couldn't keep any of it down.

Vern Gosney, who had left his five-year-old son behind when he escaped from Jonestown, had been hit in the chest. He wailed and screamed throughout the night.

Steve Sung, the NBC sound man, astonished us by getting up on his feet the following morning. I thought he was nearly well. But he turned out to be among the most seriously wounded of all.

Back at the rum house, we were treated with incredible kindness. The woman who owned the place gave us what she had—some coffee, Pepsi, beer, and bananas.

We kept paying, pushing Guyanese bills into the woman's hand. But of course it wasn't enough to pay her for the enormous risks she was taking. Nothing could compensate for that.

Several Guyanese sat in front of the hut, guarding us. They had a single knife among them.

We were terrified.

Every time a loose branch fell off a tree during the heavy, tropical storm that raged all night and clattered on the tin roof, we held our breath.

At times we thought we saw lights or heard trucks on the airstrip.

Most of us would duck back into the tall grass when this happened. But Bob Flick, the NBC producer, a big, beefy man with lots of experience in tough scrapes outside the country, just stood there in the center of the wounded.

He had stood by me during the twelve hours when I was detained at the airport by Guyanese immigration, and now he was standing firm by his injured companions.

I kept thinking, This is a real test of courage. I don't think he would have moved if a tank had come down that airstrip.

There were intervals when we could lie down. I reclined for a while on a foam rubber pillow. My arm was bloody and aching. My knee was twisted. I had a lump in my throat.

Sleep, of course, was impossible.

And time moved slowly.

By daybreak the tent where we kept our seriously wounded had the foul odor of rotting flesh. The wounded themselves could smell it, and they remarked on it.

Flies and bugs were crawling all over these people. We tried to brush them off as best we could.

And somehow Jackie Speier still was smiling whenever anyone looked at her.

At 8:30 a.m.—sixteen hours after the attack—the first Guyanese troops arrived. They were a welcome sight, those men wearing round bush hats, and tacky fatigues and carrying comforting, snub-nosed submachine guns.

They had been flown from Georgetown during the night to the lighted runway at Matthews Ridge. Then they had traveled by train most of the way to Port Kaituma, finishing their journey first by Land Rover and truck and finally covering the last few hundred yards on foot so that they wouldn't be ambushed.

We had made it after all.

Dick Dwyer ordered us back into the house while he met with the soldiers. He said he didn't want anybody to mistake us for the marauders from the Peoples Temple.

After a time Dwyer rejoined us. He went to the kitchen sink and very methodically began washing his hands.

I told him that in all the time we had been there, none of us had ever used that sink to wash up. I wondered why he was doing it now.

"I've just been stripping the dead," he replied. "It's not a very nice job."

And he produced the wallets, the combs, the money clips, the spare change—all that remained of the lives of the five who died.

The first plane didn't arrive until 10:20 a.m. It was a small black and yellow army plane that could carry five. And though it had been sent to the scene of a serious shooting, it carried no stretchers, no blankets, no first-aid supplies of any kind.

We asked the pilot why.

"This is Guyana," he replied with an embarrassed smile.

A second plane, an eighteen-seater, arrived soon afterward.

The planes waited for half an hour while we attempted to persuade the fugitives from Jonestown who had spent the night with us to get aboard.

They said no. They had too many relatives still out in the wilds, like Tom Bogue, a seventeen-year-old who had fled into the jungle clad only in a red basketball uniform, sweat socks, and tennis shoes when the firing began. That young man from Suisun, California, we learned later, had hidden out with four other young people and brought them all to safety.

Beyond that, the survivors were frightened to fly to Georgetown. They were certain that members of the Peoples Temple would be waiting at the airport, ready to shoot down the planes.

Dwyer, who had been slightly wounded in the thigh, also remained behind to continue carrying out his duties as a representative of the United States government at the departure site.

I asked him how his wound was.

"Fine," he replied.

Was there anything I could get for him or do for him at Georgetown?

"Just tell the folks at the embassy to have a cold Banks beer waiting for me," he replied.

While this report out of Guyana had the tone of war correspondence, the later information was horrific beyond belief. People sought comparisons in history. None existed.

12

ARMAGEDDON

The babies were the first to die. The cyanide was squirted into their little mouths with syringes.

Then came the older children. They lined up in the central pavilion, where Jim Jones had addressed them so many times. This time they did his bidding again. They lined up to accept cups of Kool-Aid laced with poison.

Next came their parents and the old folks. They, too, waited their turn to obey the orders to die, while armed guards stood by ready to shoot down any who tried to escape.

And—no one knows precisely when—there was the death of Jim Jones himself, killed by a single bullet in the right temple in the forty-seventh year of his life.

Jones, "the Father," had called his flock together and told them it was time to depart for heaven.

"We're going to meet," he promised, "in another place."

The words kept coming over the camp's loudspeakers.

"There is great dignity in dying. It is a great demonstration for everyone to die."

And then the final word, repeated six times: "Mother, mother, mother, mother, mother, mother."

In that awful time in the late afternoon of Saturday, November 18, over nine hundred men, women, and children perished in the settlement of Jonestown, Guyana, thousands of miles away from their homes in the United States.

The cyanide took about five minutes of kill the victims. The strongest and healthiest probably lasted a little longer.

Six miles to the east, at the Port Kaituma airstrip, the survivors of the attack that killed Congressman Leo Ryan and four others were expecting a return of the killers at any instant. Neither they nor anyone else had any idea yet of the dimensions of the disaster they were experiencing.

By the time the *Chronicle*'s Ron Javers heard the first reports, he was already in Malcolm Grove Air Force Medical Center at Andrews Air Force Base, outside Washington.

Javers, with a bullet still embedded in his left shoulder, managed to get off the Air Force Medivac plane during a fueling stop in Puerto Rico long enough to telephone the incredible account of the airstrip tragedy to the *Chronicle*.

At Andrews, he called in a report on his interviews with Jim Jones at Jonestown. Two doctors tried to pull him away from the phone, but he wouldn't budge.

Finally, it took a general to force Javers to go into the operating room. John Fogarty, the *Chronicle*'s Washington correspondent, took Javers's notebook and read the rest of his notes to a colleague in the newspaper's city room in San Francisco.

Meanwhile Keith Power, a *Chronicle* assistant city editor, had volunteered to fly to Georgetown to make sure Javers received proper care. As it turned out, the two crossed paths. Power arrived in Georgetown in time to report the rest of the story after Javers's departure. Power called in the discovery of the first 405 bodies on Monday, November 20. Authorities thought that would be the final total.

And Javers still had one additional important story to tell.

It began like this:

"When we were waiting in hope of being rescued from Port Kaituma Saturday after the death of Congressman Leo J. Ryan and four others in our group, we were told that a mass suicide was about to occur at Jonestown.

"And we were also told it was to be only the first chapter in a terrible reign of carnage."

The second chapter, Javers said, was that Jones and a few of his aides were to survive, go into hiding, smuggle themselves back into the United States, seek out their enemies, and then kill them—one by one.

Former Peoples Temple members were terror-stricken at this prospect until they learned that Jones's body, flown from Guyana in an aluminum container numbered 13-B and labeled "Rev. Jimmie Jones," had been positively identified in the morgue at Dover Air Force Base, Delaware.

It took a while to learn all the facts of the aftermath in Guyana.

Authorities announced immediately, for instance, that Sharon Amos, the forty-two-year-old woman who had seemed so pleasant when Javers visited her at the Georgetown Peoples Temple, had murdered her three children and then killed herself. Martin Amos, nine, who had played at his mother's feet while Javers interviewed her; Christa Amos, ten; and Liane Harris, twenty-one, a child of an earlier marriage, had all had their throats slashed.

Liane's father, Sherwin Harris, a big, bearded man who runs a vending machine company across the bay from San Francisco, was one of the Concerned Relatives who had flown to Georgetown with Ryan.

From the outset he called all four deaths murder. The Guyana police finally agreed, a week later, that Sharon Amos, a tiny woman, was incapable of slashing her own throat. They arrested Charles Edward Beikman, forty-three, whose association with Jim Jones dated back twenty years to the days when Jones was still dreaming of success in Indianapolis.

"He says he was helping them commit suicide," Assistant Police Commissioner C. A. Roberts said in Georgetown.

Roberts said police were able to identify Beikman because he tried unsuccessfully to kill a twelve-year-old girl who had witnessed the killings.

It would be some time before Guyana police would know how many members of the Jones cult to charge with murder.

The first to be arrested was Larry Layton, the man who fired the first shots in the Port Kaituma airstrip attack.

He was accused of killing two people, but he had really planned to destroy an entire planeload.

Layton's instructions were to pose as a Temple refugee, board Ryan's plane after the visit to Jonestown, and shoot the pilot in midair. If the plan worked, everybody would die, including Layton.

As it happened, Layton survived, only to be captured at the airstrip and charged with murder. In Guyana, murder is a capital offense punishable by hanging.

Michael Prokes, thirty-one, once the bureau chief in Stockton, California, for a Sacramento television station, was arrested a few days later when he was discovered near the airstrip.

Prokes, a former Christian Scientist and a deeply religious man, had interviewed Jones in

1972 and was so taken by him that he gave the evangelist his life's savings of $7,000 and went to work as the assistant pastor of the Peoples Temple in San Francisco.

Tim Carter, thirty, formerly of Garden City, Idaho, was arrested with Prokes. *Chronicle* reporter George Draper discovered that Carter had flown up to San Francisco to scout out the Ryan visit in advance and name the members of the Ryan group.

Other names turned up. Fugitives from Jonestown who survived the airstrip raid knew the identities of their attackers.

There was more information from the few survivors of Jonestown. Odell Rhodes, thirty-six, a former teacher, escaped because the camp's doctor, Lawrence Schacht, asked him to fetch a stethoscope after Schacht and the colony's nurses had made their cyanide brew.

Rhodes left on the errand as requested, but he didn't return. Instead, he found a nearby refuge in the jungle, where he could view and hear the terrible scene.

It was Rhodes who reported that it took five minutes for the cyanide to do its work—time enough for families to reunite with arms entwined about one another before dying.

Only one woman protested, Rhodes said, and she was shouted down for daring to disobey the orders of "Father."

Among the others who survived Jonestown was Grover Davis, who at seventy-nine had the sense to run away and hide in the brush. The other was Hyacinth Prash, a white-haired woman who stayed in her dormitory bed because she was too sick to get up and attend the ghastly ceremonies.

Two others who got out of Jonestown were lawyers Charles Garry and Mark Lane, who had stayed behind when Ryan climbed into the dump truck for the ride to the Port Kaituma airstrip.

The two men, bitterly angry at each other throughout much of the visit, were forced to work together when they prevented Donald Sly from cutting Ryan's throat at Jonestown.

As a San Francisco member of Peoples Temple, which kept proclaiming itself a nonviolent sect, Sly was known for enlivening the services by screaming, "Kill 'em all, kill 'em all!"

Lane and Garry had even more incentive to become friends, at least temporarily, when they were led to a hut near the Jonestown pavilion just before the mass deaths were to begin.

They said they saw eight men carrying automatic rifles and ammunition and two other armed guards outside their hut.

"They said to us with smiles on their faces, 'We are all going to die,'" Lane later told reporters at Georgetown. "They were relaxed and happy, and I wondered if they were not doped."

Lane said he offered the soldiers some parting words of comfort.

"I told them, 'At least Garry and I will be able to tell the story,'" Lane continued. "They hugged us and said good-bye."

The lawyers said they ran off into the jungle. They turned up at Port Kaituma after the Guyanese troops arrived.

By then the chief problem remaining was to account for five hundred or more residents of the colony who were still apparently missing. American military spokesmen said there couldn't be that many in the jungle. If they were, they would have left tracks.

But there were eight or nine hundred American passports in Jones's office at the settlement. And there didn't seem to be any more graves. Where was everybody?

The terrible answer was learned on Friday. The American army crews who came, at the insistence of Guyanese authorities, to get the bodies out of the country found them piled deeper at the death scene in Jonestown than anyone had imagined.

Among the newly discovered victims were many young children.

The burial of the airstrip victims took place earlier.

Congressman Ryan's body was brought home to San Mateo County. Fifty-four congressional colleagues, a host of California political leaders, and many, many old friends filled All Souls Catholic Church in South San Francisco to capacity. Five hundred stood outside in the gray rain.

His body was put to rest next to the grave of Fleet Admiral Chester W. Nimitz in Golden Gate National Cemetery, overlooking what an aide called "the bay he loved so much"—San Francisco Bay. And though it seems improbable, the fact is that a spectacular double rainbow appeared just as the rain stopped and the mourners walked away.

Services for Greg Robinson, the twenty-seven-year-old *San Francisco Examiner* photographer, were held at St. Jude's Episcopal Church in Burbank, California, where his parents live and where he was reared. Cameraman Bob Brown of NBC received a funeral mass in St. Ambrose Church, Hollywood, and NBC news correspondent Don Harris was eulogized in the First Baptist Church in his hometown of Vidalia, Georgia.

In San Francisco, the remaining members of Peoples Temple were in shock. About forty of them gathered at the spacious temple on Geary Boulevard for Thanksgiving dinner.

They complained that they were already receiving ugly phone calls, like "Killed any children lately?" and "Everyone in that building is going to have their brains blown out."

Former members of Peoples Temple, almost all of whom had relatives who perished at Jonestown, were also in shock.

And so, it appeared, was Charles Garry, who met with the press and said he still thought Jonestown was "a noble and beautiful experiment."

"Those beautiful programs, destroyed in a matter of minutes," Garry said. "I just can't make any sense of it."

Lane the specialist in conspiracies, confided that he had known something was odd all along, but he had kept it from Garry.

According to Garry, Lane knew about the suicide plans that Jones had in case of a final disaster to the cult. But, according to Lane, several U.S. agencies, including the State Department,

CIA, and FBI were also aware of the cult's suicide plans.

Lane and other in the group had heard rumors that there were plans to lace the grilled cheese sandwiches served to Ryan's party at the Peoples Temple settlement with tranquilizers or other drugs.

"I brought along some cough drops, which have a lot of sugar in them," Lane said. "I sure as hell wasn't going to eat the cheese sandwiches."

Javers ate one. He said he had heard the rumors too. But neither he nor anyone else in the group had a sense of being drugged.

Garry was outraged. If Lane had shared his knowledge, Garry insisted, the disaster could have been prevented, either by talking Jones out of it or by alerting the Guyanese authorities.

Through it all, the survivors were trying to explain their situation—even if they couldn't make sense out of it.

They were joined by commentators throughout the world.

The Vatican's *Osservatore Romano* spoke of "the futility of a pseudomysticism which betrays the cause of man because it betrays the cause of Christ."

TASS reported in Moscow that it saw the Peoples Temple—which Jones described as a socialist colony sympathetic to the Soviets—as "a symptom of the notorious American way of life."

In Paris, *Le Monde* said Jones had to transport his followers away from the United States and isolate them in order to carry out his plan. But most of the rest of the press was less kind.

The *Journal de Genève* in Switzerland, for instance, said, "Although it took place in South America, this terrifying story belongs to the United States. Waves of religious feeling are apparently a constant of American history."

"Is there anything hidden in California that brings out such lunacy?" demanded a columnist of Tokyo's *Asahi Shimbun.*

"American society is composed of joiners, of people who like to form associations," said the *Süddeutsche Zeitung* of Munich, where a bunch of joiners got together after World War I and formed the National Socialist party.

The comments from the press were interesting, but the greatest impact came in the words of those closest to the scene.

"I can almost say I hate the man," said Jones's nineteen-year-old son Stephan, who escaped the Jonestown killings because he was in Georgetown with the colony's basketball team.

"He has destroyed almost everything I have lived for."

EPILOGUE
WHY?

by Herb Caen

I

The vocabulary of horror stretches only so far. In the case of the Reverend Jim Jones and Peoples Temple, the words—those "buzz" words so dear to the heart of every newspaper headline writer—soon ran out of steam and meaning. *Bizarre* and *grotesque* were followed by *nightmare* and *shock*. The unbelievable became all too real, and the unspeakable was at last given tongue and voice. Then came stunned silence, the only possible response to the still-unanswered question: Why?

The last chapter remains to be written, if it can be written, but the penultimate chapter emerged from deadline to deadline as a "story," in the newspaper sense of the word. And as a story it was, for once, worthy of being called unique. Journalists and sociologists, professional and amateur, pored over their typewriters and spoke into microphones, attempting to invoke comparisons. And failing.

The mounds of bodies in the jungle stillness of Guyana, dead of a nightmare mixture of Kool-Aid and cyanide, reminded some observers of the brave Jews of Masada who killed themselves in their fortress rather than surrender to the Roman legions. The analogy is not apt; the Jews knew they were going to die in any case. The ghosts of Buchenwald and Auschwitz were summoned, but failed to materialize; concentration camps were part of official German policy, not the whim of an isolated leader.

All manner of cults and cultists were discussed, in print and during the inevitable talk shows, but from the Reverend Moon to Esalen, from communism to fascism and back again, nothing and nobody seems to provide a final clue to the mystery of the Reverend Jim Jones. His almost religious and definitely mystical power, its evil well concealed, must somehow be construed as a clue to the mystery that is the 1970s. But the meaning remains hidden by masks of personal motives, distant, exotic regions, and, finally, death.

II

"The story." I keep returning to that journalistic phrase because it was in the newspapers that Jim Jones made his first impact on the public consciousness, and it was in their pages that he became a controversial figure, admired and wooed by some, vilified and mocked by others.

He used the press and was used by it. He seemed fascinated and repelled by publicity, often saying, "Don't write about me, write about my people and what they are trying to accomplish." During his years in San Francisco, his name appeared in the newspapers with increasing frequency, and he began reacting with increasing nervousness. He had something to conceal from the glare of publicity, but nobody knew what it was then.

In the early days of Peoples Temple, the media found him to be "a charismatic figure" who exerted "considerable clout" in politics. He became the "madman" of Guyana only in the dark, dying days of his dynasty. By the same token, his followers turned "fanatical," in the estimation of the media, as they crumpled in the convulsions of cyanide. Until then they had been "dedicated followers," perhaps misguided but seeking a better life and hence deserving of sympathy.

In the flamboyant San Francisco of the early 1970s, Jim Jones emerged slowly from obscurity. It was a time when a colorful and outgoing preacher, the Reverend Cecil Williams, was attracting national attention with his Sunday services at Glide Memorial Church in San Francisco's Tenderloin district. Cecil Williams loved the spotlight and made no bones about it. He pulled together celebrities and hippies, rock stars and dopers, Hell's Angels and socialites into services that were theatrical in the extreme. He could say with reason that he was putting on "the best show in town," and if you wanted a seat on a Sunday morning at Glide, you had to get there early.

Jim Jones seemed a refreshing contrast to Cecil Williams and his "Let's boogie!" approach to ecumenism. Nevertheless, Jim, as he asked people to call him almost immediately, was courting attention too, in a different way.

I first became aware of him in 1972, when I wrote a small item in my *San Francisco Chronicle* column about a neighborhood florist who had performed a kind deed for a person in distress. The next day I received a check for $1000 made out to the florist, along with a letter from Jim Jones. He wrote: "At Peoples Temple, we are pleased to learn about those who help their fellow man, without thought of recompense or reward. When we hear about such acts of kindness, we rejoice that goodness survives in a world that is, in so many ways, wicked. Please convey this check to the florist with our thanks. We will continue to follow your column, and the newspaper in general, to find other examples of deeds that deserve support from Peoples Temple."

The florist, a young man on the shorts, cashed the check without much hope that it would clear. When it did, he was dizzy with delight —and mystified. I, too, was mystified and fascinated. I discovered Peoples Temple in a former Masonic Temple on Geary Boulevard, flanked by the original Fillmore Auditorium, where the rock scene first flourished in San Francisco, and by a Kentucky Fried Chicken franchise. The neighborhood was predominantly black. I checked around among the black politicians and was told that "Jim Jones is a terrific guy, a real leader, a man the ghetto people can believe in. He is going to be a real force in this city. You should take time to meet him."

III

Jim Jones agreed to meet me for lunch on the condition that I would not interview him, or quote him, but would write about the aims of his group. I found him a rather attractive, enigmatic personality, soft-spoken and shy, becoming voluble only on the subject of "helping those who cannot help themselves." He looked part American-Indian, as he claimed to be, and wore a black, almost ascetic "uniform"—a sort of Mao jacket with matching pants. He seldom smiled and had no discernible sense of humor. During the two luncheon meetings we had, he was accompanied by a thin, intense young man named Mike Prokes, an aide who acted as press secretary, in effect, and who seemed completely devoted to "Jim."

Peoples Temple was not a story that fit comfortably into the kind of anecdotal column I write, but I did print a couple of short items, such as the usual $1000 check to the florist, that presented the Temple in a favorable light. The reaction was unnerving, to say the least. Dozens of letters poured into the *Chronicle*, praising me for my kindness and extolling Jones. The letters were almost identical, in handwriting ranging from neat to illiterate. Obviously, they had been ordered by Jim Jones and their contents dictated. I backed away from the story to await further developments.

They were not long in coming. For all its diversity, San Francisco is a comparatively small town, and anyone who can deliver a solid bloc of votes—2000, say, enough to swing an election—is certain to be wooed by politicians. Liberals and "progressives" of every stripe camped on Jones's doorstep and ingratiated themselves with his followers. Mayor George Moscone then claimed Jones for his very own by appointing him to the Housing Commission. He was swiftly confirmed, even by those conservative politicians at City Hall who now decry the "gullible liberals who must share the blame for this tragedy."

As Jones emerged from obscurity, so did his enemies. Dissidents and detractors began spreading stories that made him appear to be, not the humanitarian he seemed, but a harsh taskmaster, a cruel man, a liar and cheat, potentially dangerous. Jones denied the charges. Mike Prokes denounced the attacks as "scurrilous, the work of small and demented minds." The mayor and his political supporters refused to believe the anti-Jones stories. "Jim Jones is a good man," one told me. "Until his critics can come up with some hard evidence—a 'smoking gun'—we will continue to believe he is exactly what he seems to be."

Nevertheless, the aura of Jim Jones began changing rapidly, and for the worse. As the rumors grew stronger, some politicians began backing off. Marshall Kilduff investigated the charges of the dissidents and believed them. Jones and Mike Prokes became more frantic in their denials. Then Kilduff and Phil Tracy wrote a story about Peoples Temple for *New West* magazine, and the world of Jim Jones began collapsing.

Instead of refuting the charges, instead of thundering his denials, he retreated. Although few people knew it then, he and his followers were getting ready to leave San Francisco for his final retreat to Guyana. There he would be welcome, secure, and free from criticism. There he would create the perfect society. The government of Guyana was delighted to have him. Some of the most eminent of American political figures had already written letters commending Jim Jones. Surely a president's wife and United States senators could not be mistaken.

I found his decision to leave the country utterly mystifying. It was at around that time that I ran across an odd story of how Jim Jones had fathered a son by the estranged wife of a Peoples Temple member. It was a rather scandalous story, but amply documented, and was to become important in future developments. Whenever I asked the Peoples Temple lawyer, Charles Garry, why Jones did not return to answer the charges of his critics, Garry would assure me, "He loves that little boy too much. Can't you understand his predicament? He is afraid that if he returns, he will lose custody of the child to the mother and her husband, both of whom are deadly enemies of Jim Jones. I have advised him to stay where he is until this matter is settled."

IV

The "explanation" sounded preposterous. By remaining in Guyana with his followers, he was only confirming the worst that was being said and printed about him. Now he was described openly as a madman, a megalomaniac, a paranoiac, and a potential killer. His supporters, especially those politicians who had benefited from his power, continued to say, "Jim will come back and straighten all this out." (Translation: "We couldn't possibly have been wrong about him.") Garry continued to say coolly, "He'll return when I tell him to." Nothing made sense. So I wrote to Jim Jones at Jonestown in Guyana and asked him why he was remaining in exile as his name was being blackened.

On April 3, 1978, he replied in a long, strangely eloquent letter. "I felt and still feel," he wrote, "that it is necessary to protect my child from being used as a pawn by people who have no real interest in him." (He also spoke of his fear that Peoples Temple would lose its tax exemption over his having fathered a child out of wedlock, "an act against the beliefs of the Disciples," his sect.)

"All my life," he went on, "I have endured the pain of poverty, and suffered many disappointments and heartaches common to humankind. For that reason, I try to make others happy and secure. So many who are suffering are not happy unless they see others suffering as well. Perhaps that is why I have tried so hard to compensate for that factor, and make this society a joyous one that celebrates life."

When I replied that he had evaded the question of why he did not return to San Francisco, he wrote that his place was with his people, the last of his followers. "For many years," he said, "I have existed on the premise that I am needed, because long ago I realized what a cruel hoax life is, how false illusions are, how unjust. Even here in Guyana, a place of great physical beauty and tremendous potential, I am not 'happy.' It is too much of a responsibility to be the administrator of this socialistic society. But even if I did not have this on my shoulders, I doubt I could ever be happy knowing that two-thirds of the world's children have no future but the prospect of lives 'nasty, brutish and short.'

"I think I will always bear the guilt of knowing that this model socialistic society should have been built in the United States. Perhaps, if I had communicated somehow differently, I could have exposed those liars who have so callously tried to ruin what has been for many people the only chance they had to make something out of their lives. . . . Many of the young people who came here were alienated, angry, and frustrated. They were tired of the hypocrisy that cried over 'human rights' while they were being buried alive. . . . The society we are building in Guyana has given people who were considered the refuse of urban America a new sense of pride, self-worth, and dignity."

Surely not, on the surface, the words of a madman on the verge of *Götterdämmerung*. Nothing there to forewarn Congressman Leo Ryan and his entourage of media people that they were walking into a death trap. Perhaps, in retrospect, there was a more tangible clue to the ultimate disaster in the last letter I received from Mike Prokes.

On the letterhead stationery of the Peoples Temple Agricultural Mission in Jonestown, Guyana, it reads in part:

"They will never destroy what we have, because we made the determination long ago that if they came after one of us, they would have to take us all on. Martin Luther King perhaps said it best: 'A man who hasn't found something to die for isn't fit to live.' Well, we've found something to die for and it's called . . . social justice. So it doesn't matter what they succeed in doing to us or how we are finally portrayed. We at least will have the satisfaction of living that principle, not because it promised success or reward, but simply because it was the right thing to do—the highest way we knew to live our lives."

V

Already Mike Prokes was writing in the past tense. Upon rereading his letter, I see, in retrospect, that he was quite capable of killing himself for Jim Jones—or even killing for Jim Jones. Here was the fine madness, the shining idealism of so many people who, throughout history, have tried to change life to conform more closely to their vision, shared or otherwise.

And so the great world came to Jim Jones in the jungle. It came in a familiar form—the media on the trail of "the story" that now will take its place in history. Even near the end, the press was not aware of what it was getting into. Perhaps the best illustration of this can be found in these words by Charles Krause of the *Washington Post,* himself wounded in the airstrip massacre: "What had started as a zany story about a Congressman wanting to investigate a freaky religious commune in Guyana was no longer zany."

"Zany," "freaky,"—the typical verbiage of the media "event" that began so lightheartedly and ended in the unforgettable grotesquerie of mass suicide by Kool-Aid laced with cyanide;

the summer drink and the winter death, presided over by the Emperor Jones of the Jungle.

In Eugene O'Neill's great play, the Emperor Jones becomes the victim of his—and mankind's—aboriginal fears. Jim Jones and his followers in death were consumed by their own fears, too, retreating from the jungle of the urban ghetto to the jungle of the tropics, dying miserable deaths without a word that would give some meaning to the disaster.

The cause for which they died remains unspoken. Thus they died in vain, and that is the ultimate tragedy.

San Francisco
November 25, 1978

ABOUT THE AUTHORS

RON JAVERS, 32 years old, came to the *San Francisco Chronicle* as a special projects writer in January, 1978, where his first assignment was analyzing Proposition 13 and the taxpayer revolt.

Before that he spent six years at the *Philadelphia Daily News* where he was news editor, op-ed page columnist, editorial writer, editorial page editor, and, finally, associate editor.

Javers has won both national and local awards for his writing and reporting, and in 1975-76 he was a Nieman Fellow at Harvard University. His articles and book reviews have appeared in *Commonweal*, the *Philadelphia Inquirer*, the *Boston Globe* and *Philadelphia* magazine.

He lives in San Francisco with his wife, Eileen, and their two children.

MARSHALL KILDUFF, a 29-year-old native of San Francisco, joined the staff of the *San Francisco Chronicle* after graduating from Stanford University in 1971. He has covered education, urban affairs and the San Francisco mayor's office for the paper.

In 1976 he was given an award by the Associated Press for a story on the "Pink Palace" housing project—an idea which was indirectly given to him by Rev. Jim Jones.

Mr. Kilduff's articles have also appeared in *New West* and *Rolling Stone* magazines.

HERB CAEN, 62, is a native of Sacramento, California. He has been writing a column six days a week for the *San Francisco Chronicle* for four decades and he is the recognized authority on the life and style of that city. He has written ten books about his favorite ctiy and numerour articles have appeared in *Playboy, Esquire, The Saturday Evening Post, Holiday* and *Reader's Digest.*

Caen lives with his wife, Maria Theresa, and their son, in the Bay Area.